KHANTASTIC

Praise for the book

Meticulously researched and packed with lesser-known nuggets from the Khans' fascinating success stories, *KHANtastic* puts into sharp perspective why these three men from the 'Bandra Triangle' may well be the last bonafide superstars to come out of Bollywood. Sanjukta Nandy casts an honest, unvarnished eye on their respective trajectories to discover why this trio, linked by fate, was destined to leave an indelible imprint on Indian film culture. This book is a breezy, enjoyable read...like some of their best films.

—Rajeev Masand, film critic

KHANtastic is a treasure trove of anecdotes and trivia, and strong on perspective and storytelling. It is an absolute 'fan-tribute' to a phenomena that has practically defined and dominated desi pop culture for three decades, and continues to do so!

—Mayank Shekhar, film critic,
journalist and author

KHANTASTIC

The Untold Story of Bollywood's Trio

SANJUKTA NANDY

RUPA

Published by
Rupa Publications India Pvt. Ltd 2020
7/16, Ansari Road, Daryaganj
New Delhi 110002

Sales Centres:
Allahabad Bengaluru Chennai
Hyderabad Jaipur Kathmandu
Kolkata Mumbai

ISBN: 978-93-5333-769-8

First impression 2020

10 9 8 7 6 5 4 3 2 1

The moral right of the author has been asserted.

Printed at Replika Press Pvt. Ltd, India

For my dad,
Forever in my heart, you teach me to
dream on from even beyond the stars.

Contents

Introduction

Why KHANtastic?

Spring of 1988. My annual exams at school were over. Lazing in my balcony, I was suddenly shocked to see our neighbour's son return home with dishevelled hair and a torn shirt. The young man happened to be part of an enthusiastic fan club that had grown around a boy named Raj who had gained cult status from the film, *Qayamat Se Qayamat Tak*. On that particular day, our neighbour's son had been bestowed with a darshan of his idol, but not without enduring the mean end of a lathi from the police. This matinee idol, Raj, was none other than Aamir Khan. Aamir, too, had lost his shirt that day, torn by admirers who were struggling to grab a piece of the new-age poster boy.

Fast forward to the next year. Come 18 January 1989, every Wednesday, my cousins and I used to wait eagerly to watch a particular TV series, *Fauji*. We had moved our dinner time to ensure that the serial was not missed and the midweek prime-time slot was allotted to a certain Lieutenant Abhimanyu Rai. This budding actor/commando who had grabbed our attention and hijacked our dinner time was a young actor from Delhi—Shah Rukh Khan.

Post my winter vacation of 1989, I could barely concentrate in my Mathematics class, as a few backbencher classmates hovered over a postcard that was being passed around the room. Just as the postcard reached the student seated next to me, our teacher arrested this game of Pass the Parcel. But I had already peeped into the parcel, which bore the picture of a young, large-eyed actor with a signature running across it—'Love…Salman'. Though we stood with our nose to the wall that day, it didn't deter certain enthusiasts from pasting large posters of Salman Khan on their bedroom walls and whispering '*Maine Pyar Kiya*'.

I went on to study Architecture and then practise Design. But there was something magnetic about the Khans that never allowed me to take my mind off them. It was as if they were following me through their films, stories, newspaper articles, interviews and various other escapades. The three Khans were by now gaining the status of the Holy Trinity, thanks to their humungous fan following.

So off I went to meet friends, colleagues, and near and dear ones who have known the Khans as mortal beings, and those who would help me delve deeper into their personal stories which were yet unknown to the outside world.

Did Shah Rukh Khan initially reject *Dilwale Dulhania Le Jayenge*?

Did *Lagaan* nearly get scrapped because of Aamir?

Was Salman the reason why Shah Rukh's mansion, Mannat, stands tall?

Each of their stories, as narrated in this book, is like a film script, with extraordinary ups and downs, raw brotherhood and fights, adulation and criticism, which together sum up a stupendous journey that rolls on with unexpected twists and turns.

And the best part of this story is that their journey is still current, because, '*Picture abhi baaki hai mere dost* (The story isn't over yet).'

Sanjukta Nandy

Prologue

A Momentous Iftar Party

21 July 2013. Taj Lands End, Mumbai
Baba Siddique's Iftar Party

The sky was cloudy and the sea breeze blew strongly into the stiffly starched uniforms of the gatekeepers. The fancy cars waited bumper to bumper for their turn to drop off their well-heeled passengers. The ambience outside the Bandra five-star hotel echoed with glitz and glamour.

Inside the ballroom, the gathering buzzed over a lavish spread of kebabs, mutton samosas, paneer tikkas, roti pe botis and desserts such as shahi tukda, rabdi and malpua. And yet there was this palpable undercurrent of immense tension.

The time of the main event mentioned on the iftar invite was 7.22 p.m. All the guests were aware that it would be attended by two Bollywood stars, stalwarts in their own right but at extreme warring ends of the spectrum. The duo was known to have had a strong brotherhood until that one fateful night, when everything changed between them. They had not met face to face for over five years following an unpleasant end to a certain birthday bash at the Olive Bar & Kitchen in Mumbai.

One of the celebrities invited to the party, a Badshah in

his own right, dressed in black, walked in and made himself comfortable. As he sat at one end of the long table, chatting graciously with the other guests, the uber-cool Bhai of Bollywood walked in.

Dressed in a snug salmon-coloured tee and accompanied by the host, he courteously greeted the chief minister of Maharashtra, who was also present at the event. He then moved on to speak to the other guests. As the Being Human superstar moved closer to where the other gentleman-star sat, there was a palpable strain of edginess in the air. The guests waited with bated breath, imagining the worst to follow.

The Khan in the tee passed the King in the black outfit, and then suddenly turned back. He tapped the friend on his shoulder. The other Khan turned from his plate and looked up. What followed was history—A momentous embrace between the estranged 'brothers'. A thundering applause that refused to die down. And a picture that made for a thousand headlines and was fodder for many a media byte for months.

The host, Baba Siddique, a prominent politician in Maharashtra, later mentioned that it indeed was the hand of God that had got the two friends back together again on the auspicious occasion of Ramzan, the sacred month of fasting and prayer in Islam.

As the breaking news reached far and wide, a few corners down the venue, another versatile Khan smiled for his friends. All was well.

The duel was over and the trio was back...

Sanjukta Nandy

Destiny's Children

Aamir

As the rain lashed outside, a five-month-old baby lay lifeless. Hearing the mother and the child's ayah scream for help, the father, Tahir, ran into the house and found that the child was not breathing. On the ayah's suggestion, Tahir gave his son artificial respiration for five minutes. Finally, little Aamir stirred and was immediately rushed to the hospital.

Described by his father as a child who was undemanding and mature for his age, little Mohammed Aamir Hussain Khan grew up to be the leader of the Time Pass Gang. He stayed busy playing with his gang and siblings, cycling around the apartment complex on the bicycle that his mother had brought for him, flying kites, organizing fairs, inviting others to join their group, with the hope to head this little enterprise to an eventful success. When not busy with his gang, he was a voracious reader. At the age of six, he finished reading his first Enid Blyton and as he grew up, most of his pocket money was lavished on books. Author and film-maker Alfred Hitchcock and fictional characters in mystery book series such as *Hardy Boys* and *Nancy Drew* became an integral part of his childhood before he moved on to read humourists such as P.G. Wodehouse and classics by Charles Dickens and Leo Tolstoy. Even as an eight-year-old, he was most attracted by not only storybooks but also the very art of storytelling, and this was his closely guarded secret.

Little Mohammed Aamir, as described by his family, was a thoughtful young boy and a combination of shyness and mischief formed a vital part of his persona. When he wanted his younger siblings, Faisal and Farhat, to run errands for him, he would make up a competition to see who could be the first one to get him a glass of water. He was also very close to his cousin Mansoor and his ferocious Alsatians and Golden Retriever. In fact, often when Aamir walked back from his uncle Nasir Hussain's bungalow to his apartment next door, one of the dogs would keep a watchful eye on him. Though he was not allowed to keep pets at home, little Aamir always adopted varied pets that would be a part of his life. Later in life, it was once a cobra that he carried back from work, then a dog he named Pebbles, again from work, to Chhoti, Peanuts, and the list goes on to include his present pets, the Yorkie Imli and cat Miri.

A lover of books, but not bookish, introverted at home, but a surprisingly aggressive boy at school (St Anne's in Pali Hill, where he studied till Class VIII), little Aamir once went after a boy who had hit his brother Faisal. Since then, no one dared to tease his siblings. His mother, Zeenat Hussain, was a key influence in his life. Her strong, gentle and affectionate nurturing instilled in the little sharp boy lessons on being sensitive and kind. Aamir usually won all his matches in tennis but when he would come home celebrating and jubilantly flaunting his victory, his mother would say that she was happy that Aamir had won but felt bad for the mother of the child who did not.

On one such occasion, on the tennis court in Khar Gymkhana, the twelve-year-old Aamir met a boy, Ashutosh Gowariker (who years later went on to direct Aamir in the landmark film *Lagaan,* which got nominated for the Academy Awards in 2002 for the Best Foreign Language Film). Aamir turned down Gowariker's request to play with him, saying it would spoil his game. First, Gowariker dismissed this as snobbery. Later, when he watched the twelve-year-old play, he could not help but admire Aamir's mastery over the game.

Penchant for Sports and Storytelling

Aamir's dedication to tennis was intense. He never missed a single practice session, even during the month of Ramzan when he was fasting. This absolute focus made him the under-14 state tennis champion for Maharashtra during his school years.[1] Not only in tennis, young Aamir excelled in whatever he set his mind to. Like many children of his age, he spent time solving the Rubik's cube. But unlike most children of his age, he took his hobby to a whole new level of competition and endeavoured to break the world record. He roped in his younger sister, Farhat, as his timekeeper, promising to give her credit once he achieved this feat. Whether it was chess or the Rubik's cube, Aamir's mind once set on a goal, was immovable.

The shy Aamir though, had a dream that he nurtured and kept as a well-guarded secret till he reached Class XII. He

---

[1]Lata Khubchandani, 'Aamir played national level tennis', Rediff.com, 10 March 2005, accessed 9 September 2019, https://www.rediff.com/movies/2005/mar/10tahir.htm

had begun work on it as a young lad without anyone really noticing it. Aamir was an observer and would discreetly be a part of the storytelling sessions that used to take place in his film-maker father's home. Initially, though Aamir's presence went largely unnoticed in such sessions, over the years, his father started to value his participation and intelligent observations. By the time Aamir was twelve, his father invited him to attend these sessions and encouraged him to share his opinions and reflections.

Little did the father know then that his second-born, who came into their life on 14 March 1965, at Holy Family Hospital would one day feature on the list of *Time* magazine's 100 Most Influential People in the World.[2]

Shah Rukh

It was a complicated birth. The baby had the umbilical cord looped around his neck. Though the condition has often been known to be severe, even leading to death, the baby emerged unscathed. A nurse interpreted the deadly cord around his neck as a blessing of Hanuman, the monkey-god. The child, she predicted, would be very lucky one day.

This boy, born to Meer Taj Mohammad and Lateef Fatima Khan in Delhi, was named Abdul Rehman by his nani (maternal grandmother), who adopted him and moved to Mangalore.

---

[2]*Time*, 'The 2013 TIME 100', 18 April 2013, accessed 13 September 2019, http://time100.time.com/2013/04/18/time-100/slide/aamir-khan/

His maternal grandfather, Iftekhar Ahmed, was credited with a huge contribution in building the Mangalore port.

Finding Love Amidst Drama

Born into an illustrious family of Pashtun descent, Abdul Rehman's paternal grandfather, Meer Jan Muhammad Khan, was from Peshawar, Afghanistan, hailing from an area known as the Qissa Khawani Bazaar or more famously, the Piccadilly of Central Asia. This 'marketplace of the storytellers' was the birthplace of many a doyen of the Hindi film industry such as Prithviraj Kapoor and Dilip Kumar. Romance and drama ran in their blood. Even the boy's father, Meer Taj Mohammad, the youngest child of his parents, who was sent to study Law in Delhi after the Partition of India in 1947, unexpectedly found love amidst drama.

At India Gate, Delhi, one evening, post dinner, when Meer Taj was taking a stroll with his cousin, Shah Nawaz of the Azad Hind Fauj, the unexpected happened. Their quiet saunter was interrupted by the screeching of a car that had met with an accident and had turned upside down right in front of them. The chivalrous Pathans immediately ran to the rescue of the victims.

The driver ran away, leaving behind the bleeding victims, Iftekhar Ahmed and his two daughters. The older daughter, Lateef Fatima, was severely injured. She was rushed to the hospital. She had lost her memory and needed immediate blood transfusion. Meer Taj, the eligible donor, immediately volunteered and saved Fatima's life. As she was being nursed back to health in the hospital, he would visit her every day with food and they got talking. Fatima went back to Mangalore and Meer Taj followed her there. As destiny would have it, it was the time when Fatima's mother fell ill and Meer Taj again donated blood to her. An indebted Iftekhar asked Meer Taj what he could do in return of the favour. Meer Taj promptly asked for the hand of his daughter, Fatima, in marriage. Iftekhar was in a dilemma, as Fatima was then engaged to another. But Iftekhar kept his promise to Meer Taj. Fatima was married to Meer Taj in 1959.

Born on 2 November 1965, their son, Abdul Rehman, for the first five years, grew up with his maternal family in Mangalore and then with his parents in Delhi. Once in Delhi, Meer Taj renamed him. The name meant a prince-like face, and rhymed with his elder daughter, Shehnaz Lalarukh's name—Shah Rukh.

But, growing up in the city of Delhi, where most people are fondly called by their chedds, or nicknames, Shah Rukh had one too. Usually, if someone is plump, they might be called Aloo or if someone is sweet, they might be called Pinni. As Shah Rukh was known for his swift stride and love for sports, he was fondly called Mail Gaddi or Mela.

Little Shah Rukh was a naughty five-year-old and often did things that stretched beyond his father's imagination. One day when their neighbour's sixteen-year-old daughter complained to Meer saab that his son would regularly blow her kisses and loudly greet her with 'Hi, sweetheart!' he was taken aback. An ardent admirer of the Frontier Gandhi and also known as Badshah Khan, Meer saab was a gentle and well-mannered man. He was certain that the whole episode of Shah Rukh teasing their neighbour was a mistake. He was confident that the culprit was none other than his neighbour's elder son, Subhash. So certain was he of this mistaken identity that he asked the girl to come home and called out to his five-year-old boy. Out came a spunky little boy, with bright eyes and a buoyant gait. Meer saab was certain now that the confusion would be cleared. As soon as the five-year-old Shah Rukh saw the girl, he promptly blew kisses, saying, 'Hi, sweetheart!' with a dimpled smile. The father, embarrassed, did not know what to do.

Little did the father know then that his zestful boy would harness this irrepressible charm to earn the title of Bollywood's King of Romance, the second-richest actor in the world[3] and 'the biggest movie star you've never heard of...' by Steven Zeitchik of the *Los Angeles Times* in 2011[4].

Salman

The 6.5-pound baby boy, born in Kalyanmal Nursing Home, Indore, on 27 December 1965, was sharp, active and winced at the slightest sound. His aunt, Sufiya Khan, noticed that even as an infant, he had opened his eyes right after birth. Unlike most infants, he—Abdul Rashid Salim Salman—would gaze around, as if he had come to survey the world.

Salman spent his early days in Indore with cousins, climbing trees, plucking fruits, walking in the woods and riding his bicycle for hours in the bright afternoon of the city. Indore taught him to hold the reins of a horse cart, bond with his friends and spend hot summer evenings in a madhushala—that's what sugar cane juice parlours were called in Indore then. At the age of

[3]Kounteya Sinha, 'Shah Rukh Khan second richest actor in the world', ETimes, 21 May 2014

[4]Accessed 13 September 2019, https://latimesblogs.latimes.com/movies/2011/11/shah-rukh-khan-ra-one-bollywood.html

twelve, he could jump up to 3 metres on wheels. He could take his bicycle through stony paths and even balance it on stairs. Bombay, now Mumbai, taught the boy deeper lessons. Always bright and lively, he was full of ideas and initiative.

One Diwali night, as fireworks lit up the city, Salman and his siblings were on to something unique. Imagining it to be crackers, they were rolling up paper and setting it on fire. When they ran out of paper, they wondered what to do next. 'Eureka!' said the eldest boy and reassured his siblings that he had a plan. He promptly got a bundle of paper from his father's drawer and the thrilled kids set it on fire, and the fun continued. This bundle which they set on fire was the rolled-up notes of their father's entire salary of ₹750.

When the father, Salim Khan, became aware that his entire salary had been used up as Diwali crackers, his reaction was as extraordinary as that of his first-born's imagination. Instead of a furious outburst, coupled with severe punishments, the father patiently explained to his children the importance of money and how it is the means to get food at home. That day, the eldest boy, Salman, learnt a big lesson about the importance of money and he promised never to forget it.

Time passed. One day, the principal of St Stanislaus High School, Bandra, approached his students with a request. He asked each of them to take one of the underprivileged students of the class for a meal home, so that they could experience family warmth and good food. Little Salman was the first to volunteer. Not just one, the golden-hearted boy, took seven of his classmates home for regular meals then on. His family too welcomed them to their residence, Mughal Room, with open arms. Salim saab always believed *'Mehmaan tumpe ehsaan karta hai, apni kismet ka khana tumhari table pe aake khata hai* (The guest obliges by coming to eat with you. He brings onto your table his own destiny and shares it with you).' Salman learnt the joy of giving from his father.

Salma, the Anchor

As large-hearted as he was, young Salman was a mischievous brat too. Ganesh was a guest who visited the Khan household often. Salim saab soon noticed that during these visits, Ganesh received way more importance and attention than him in his own house. Whenever Ganesh visited, he would be served tea, coffee, snacks, lunch. Wondering what made this man so special, he asked his wife, Salma, if Ganesh was related to them in some way. To his surprise, she said, 'He's the one who leaks the question papers for our sons and that's why the special treatment.'

Salma, whose maiden name was Sushila Charak, was the anchor to the entire brat pack, especially Salman. She was the friend, while his father was the disciplinarian. Salma was very inclined to sports and that's where Salman picked up his love for physical fitness and bodybuilding.

A loving boy, Salman always bonded with his family and extended family. Cousin Mubin Khan, his playmate, remembers the countless times they fell while attempting dangerous stunts on their bicycle, often breaking it altogether. But the bruises could never deter Salman from taking risks. Life in the wild, playing and being carefree always intrigued him more than academics. This landed him in trouble with his father. He was sent away to one of the top-notch boarding institutions, The Scindia School, in Gwalior. His writer-father was keen that son Salman focused on academics while he, Salim Khan, gained popular grounds in the Mumbai film industry as one of the upper crust writers.

One evening in 1975, on the eve of Independence Day celebrations, Salim saab took Salman and his brother, Arbaaz, to the premiere of a film at Minerva Cinema. The movie was co-written by him with Javed Akhtar. It had broken all records and had turned into a classic. The movie was none other than *Sholay*. Salman and Arbaaz attended this event in their Scindia School blazers, the school from where Salman completed his primary studies, before joining St Stanislaus High School in Mumbai.

Little had father Salim Khan known then that the baton of his success would be carried further by his mischievous first-born who would go on to be ranked Number 1 on Forbes Celebrity List 2016[5] and would become the Bhaijaan of a billion hearts.

The lives of three infants: Aamir Khan (born on 14 March 1965), Shah Rukh Khan (born on 2 November 1965) and Salman Khan (born on 27 December 1965), born in the same year, at different places in India and all of Pashtun descent[6], converged in the city of Bombay. They were bound by destiny to cross paths and to create cinematic milestones and unforgettable movie experiences for billions around the globe.

But not without hurdles, sweat and rejection...

---

[5]Salil Panchal and Neeraj Gangal, 'Salman Khan Tops 2016 Forbes India Celebrity 100 List', *ForbesIndia*, 23 December 2016
[6]Ancestors of Aamir Khan were descendants of Afridi Pashtuns from Qaimganj. Shah Rukh Khan's father was from Peshawar (the capital and the largest city of Khyber Pakhtunkhwa) and has Hindkowan roots. Salman Khan has his roots in the Pashtun tribe named Akuzai.

Sanjukta Nandy

2

The Bandra Boys

*Y*oung Salman was rarely without his gang of Bandra Boys, which included his neighbours and siblings. He and his friends were free spirits, habitually churning out mischievous plans. One such was silently erasing the tyre marks of Salim Khan's forbidden car.

Salim Khan was firm that the boys should not misuse his car. He had strictly forbidden them to not even touch it without his permission. The obedient nod from Salman was of a boy with a straight face but with a well-masked twinkle in the eye. Even the super-imaginative writer-father had no inkling that behind this innocent gaze was brewing an impish plan.

At the slightest opportunity, Salman would whisk off with his friends in the forbidden car, late in the night. They would, with hushed silence and measured footsteps, push the car over a hundred metres from where it was parked. Once it was well out of Salim Khan's earshot, they would ignite the engine and drive off. They would make sure to be back before daybreak and have the car parked at its original spot before their father left for his morning walk. This worked well for a few days till one day Salman left for a drive with his brother, Arbaaz, and accidentally hit the car against a pole. The dent was quite visible.

Scared, they parked the car at its usual place before their father left for his usual round in the morning. Everything looked perfectly in order and Salman was sure they had gotten away. But Salim Khan was a man with a sharp eye and soon enough caught the little mischief that his boy had parked outside their house. What happened to the Bandra Boys after that, stayed within the four walls of Galaxy Apartment forever!

Actor Dalip Tahil, who accredits his advent into the movie world to Salim saab, remembers meeting his boy, Salman. Whenever he was invited over for meals at the Khan's house, Salman, who was a shy boy, would always have a smile ready to welcome the guests. Tahil, who was then well connected and working in the advertisement world, could not help taking a liking to this young, good-looking lad.

One day Tahil informed Salim saab that the casting for Mowgli, in *The Jungle Book*, was on the roll and Salman could audition for it. Dolly Thakur, who was well known for her active participation in English theatre those days, was the key auditioner. Salman fitted the bill and tested for the role. He was not chosen though and this was the beginning of a long list of rejections for him.

For a short while, Salman was interested in taking up cricket professionally. No less than former cricketer Salim Durani was appointed as his coach. For a couple of sessions, he made it seriously to the practice but early morning schedules got to him. Waking up in the wee hours was not for Salman. He dropped out of the coaching.

Salman then decided to pursue Arts. He headed to take admission at JJ School of Arts, Mumbai. On his way, he saw the campus of St Xavier's College. The crowd out there caught his fancy and he enrolled there, in the Science faculty. This led most people close to him to believe that he intended to be a doctor or an engineer. All but one. His father was sure that Salman would be none of these. And Salim Khan was always right. Salman left college midway to join the movies.

Salman's attention then moved to actors closer home. He has often mentioned that he would admire the panache of stars such as Sanjay Dutt, Sunny Deol and Jackie Shroff and the wow effect they had on guests when they walked into any party. Salman would often wonder what he would have to do to evoke that reaction from people. He needed to crack the code. He wanted a body like Sunny Deol's, a swag like Sanjay Dutt's and cool mannerisms like those of Jackie Shroff. Salman's heart was now set on becoming a Hindi film hero.

Anand Girdhar, a small-time film-maker, was looking to cast for the title role of his film *Badnaam* in the late 1980s. Like many other aspirants, Salman headed to Girdhar's office with his portfolio, to audition for the role. Girdhar had one look at him and declined. Salman was still in his teens at that time and the film's lead role was that of a mature schoolteacher. The producer told Salman that he was too young for the role, but Salman was not one to give up. He had done a photo shoot with his friend Gautam Rajadhyaksha. The celebrity photographer was working for the advertising agency, Lintas India, and had shot Salman with a moustache and sunglasses for the clothing brand, Raymond. The young Khan was certain these pictures would do the trick for Girdhar. Results were however quite the contrary. Salman was shown the door.

This did not deter Salman. He let the rebuff work to make his focus stronger, and decided to stay behind the camera for a while. He began to assist film director Shashilal K. Nair in the film *Falak*. Salman, in those days, fostered the idea of becoming a film director. Meanwhile, his Bandra Gang was increasing in strength. The gang comprised actors Ronit Roy,

KHANtastic

Shehzad Khan, Rafiq Kazi, Iqbal, and others.

Shehzad, Salman's childhood friend and later co-star, remembers those days when the gang used to wait outside the celebrity gym at hotel Sea Rock. Stars like Sunny Deol, Amrita Singh and others would step into the gym from their fancy cars while the gang of Bandra Boys would weave dreams of being in their shoes.

By now, Salman's dream of becoming a film director had transformed since most people he met told him that he should be an actor instead. Considering it to be a unanimous vote, Salman told his father that everyone had been asking him to be in front of the camera. Pat came Salim Khan's reply, 'Who is this "everyone"? "Everyone" comes home—Ramesh Sippy, Manmohan Desai, Mahesh Bhatt... Nobody has told me this. Nobody's has told you either that "Salman beta, in my next film you're on". You see Sanjay (Dutt), Chunky (Pandey), Sunny (Deol) coming over. Do you see anything similar between them and you? You can't become a *mohalle ka dada* (street lord), lawyer or police inspector. At best you'll do a romantic film or two. What will you do after that?'

Undeterred, Salman started to work hard at bodybuilding. Noticing this, the father said, '*Yeh lo, Dara Singh banna chahta hai* (Now he wants to be Dara Singh).' Salman reacted with more hard work.

The Sea Rock gym membership was then a whopping ₹10,000 annually. Both Salim Khan and Shehzad's father, yesteryear villain, Ajit, declined to pay for the membership. The two boys then joined Bhaiya Gym in Bandra. If not anything, the gym at least had a celebrity address. It was near actor Mala Sinha's house and Dharmendra's old residence. The best part was that it had an annual fee of ₹60 only. The boys easily paid up but could not deal with what followed later.

The training was tough and the trainer was tougher on them. Shehzad dropped out but hard work did not dither Salman from putting his heart and soul into bodybuilding. His keen dedication towards fitness probably came from his athlete mother and continues till date. Even today, wherever he is shooting, Salman dedicates a good two hours to his physical training, without any exception. Bandra Physical Culture Association Gym, alias the Bhaiya Gym, established in May 1925, still stands strong on St Martin's Road and has a photo of Salman hung on its wall.

First Brush with the Camera

A chiselled body and deft swimming proved to be the stepping stone for Salman to face the camera for the first time. He has his grandmother, Badi Ammi, to thank for that. As a child when the macho man feared the thought of swimming, she told his cousins to tie Salman to a rope and toss him into the neighbourhood well. There was a turtle in the well, a big fish and a water snake. Salman was so scared that he started moving his hands and legs and swam to save his life. That was Salman's first swimming lesson.

Noted advertisement film-maker Arti Surendranath was then hunting for a model for her ad campaign. The model needed to be an expert swimmer. She noticed a well-built, fifteen-year-old boy dive into the pristine waters of Hotel Sea Rock's swimming pool in Bandra. His deft strokes and nimble swim, cutting sharply through the water, was a treat to watch. She knew her search had ended.

The next day, Salman went to meet Kailash Surendranath,

Arti's husband, who was helming the campaign. When he saw young Salman, he called Arti and said he was too young for the role. Kailash said, 'You all will look like aunties next to him.' Arti told Kailash, 'Ask him to take off his shirt.' Once the boy took off his shirt, the ad film-maker was convinced that his wife had chosen well. The spunk of the well-built boy had promise. Off he flew to the Andaman and Nicobar Islands to shoot for the Campa Cola advertisement film.

But before boarding the flight, Salman got cold feet when he saw the other glamorous and experienced models, but he held his ground with a straight face. Incidentally, his co-model happened to be Ayesha Shroff, the lady who would later marry his childhood idol, Jackie Shroff.

Those days models were not highly paid, so Salman's mother called up Kailash to find out if Salman would have to pay for his airfare and hotel stay. Kailash assured her that not only would these expenses be taken care of, but Salman would be paid for his work too. Salman received ₹17,000 for his debut in front of the camera.

All work and no play was not the vibe of the Bandra Boys. The money from the Campa Cola campaign was well spent to buy a second-hand Fiat. Shehzad fondly remembers, 'Whenever we wanted to go on drives, Salman would pool in his car while the others pooled in the petrol money. We would gather ₹25 and zoom off. Often the second-hand automobile would break down and we would run off, leaving Salman with his car, saying "*Petrol ki baat hui thi, mechanic ki nahi* (We had signed up to share the petrol money, not the mechanic's charges)".'

Young Salman was not one to let go of rambunctious pranks. In his television show, *10 Ka Dum*, he had revealed that during his youth, he had mastered the art of switching on a motorbike with his nails. He would often use that technique to take his friends' bikes for a spin without their knowledge. He would return, leaving the bike somewhere far off, just to pull a prank. When his exasperated friend would lodge a police complaint, Salman would call the police station to give them the coordinates of the bike's location.

Salman participated in all the frolic with his friends but his heart was constantly in search of that one opportunity, the next chance to face the camera. His father who had tried his hand at acting once had warned him that the path would be rough and rugged. Salim Khan made movie stars, but Salman decided he would comfortably do it on his own.

But he seemed to have forgotten that Salim Khan was always right.

Aamir, the other Khan from Bandra, was given similar advice too.

'Chacha jaan (film-maker Nasir Hussain), Abba (film producer Tahir Hussain) and Ammi felt it was a volatile profession. At that time almost everyone believed that the film industry was not a good place to be. My own family was telling me, "No. Don't go into films". Two film-makers were telling me not to enter films!' divulged Aamir at the 18th Jio MAMI Mumbai International Film Festival. Aamir's family wanted him do something 'stable'. 'One minute you are up there, the next moment you are not. There is no certainty or security. They wanted us to go into a profession that is more stable, like an engineer, doctor or chartered accountant. Anything but films.'

But Aamir had his heart fixed on films. He secretly undertook a course at the Film and Television Institute of India (FTII) in Pune, without breathing a word of it to his father or uncle. He never wanted them to feel that it was now their responsibility to launch him. 'I didn't want to ever be a burden on them,' he has stated.[7]

Little Krishna

Owing to the fear of volatility in the movie business, the family had kept Aamir away from shooting activities and the film world. There were a couple of exceptions though, when the family could not resist casting this adorable face—the face, mother Zeenat Hussain, fondly called Krishna.

The first reason to rechristen him was that he used to eat a lot of butter and the other was that, while in school, he was always surrounded by girls. Aamir used to go to the Bai Avabai Framji Petit Girls' High School in Bandra—a girls' school that allowed boys up to Class II. In Aamir's class, there were only three boys and hence, it was not unusual that they were surrounded by girls all the time. One day, when Aamir's mother was summoned to the school to attend a complaint against her naughty boy, she saw his popularity and started calling him Krishna ever since.

The first time little Krishna/Aamir was selected in a movie was to play the part of the young Shashi Kapoor. It was in Nasir Hussain's directorial venture *Pyar Ka Mausam* in 1969.

---

[7]PTI News, 'My family wanted me to be an engineer: Aamir Khan', accessed 9 September 2019, http://www.ptinews.com/news/8000485_My-family-wanted-me-to-be-an-engineer--Aamir-Khan.html

Sanjukta Nandy

The shot required for him to sit in a car, but Aamir refused. For him, sitting in anybody else's car apart from his friend Reena's, director Raj Khosla's daughter, was tantamount to being disloyal. The second time he faced the camera was for the film *Yaadon Ki Baaraat*. Directed by Nasir Hussain and co-written by none other than Salman's father, Salim Khan, the movie went on to become one of 1973's top five highest-grossing films. The film was the story of three estranged brothers and Aamir played the childhood avatar of the third brother, Ratan, who grows up to reunite them. Along with the drama, music and an ensemble star cast, the audience took home the charm of the young eight-year-old lad.

Aamir might have had the ability right from day one to tug at the heartstrings of the audience but initially, for him, a film set was a scary, dark place with small doors. 'The first time I used make-up, I really found it funny. I think they used pancake. It was wet and it felt strange. I still remember the smell of it,' he confessed years later on *Director's Cut with Kabir Bedi*.

Actor or Director?

As he grew up, young Aamir could not help being allured by the world of storytelling. He was friends with film-maker Basu Bhattacharya's son, Aditya Bhattacharya, who was also the grandson of renowned film director, Bimal Roy. At the age of sixteen, after his Class X results were declared, Aamir shot for a forty-minute short silent film called *Paranoia*, directed by his Bombay Scottish School classmate, Aditya. The film had Aamir and Neena Gupta as leads with actors Victor Banerjee and Deepa Lagoo playing Aamir's parents.

His family's dissuasion towards his aspiration made him secretive about his plans. 'Nobody in my house knew I had gone to shoot this film. I used to pretend I was going for a hockey match, but used to go for shooting,' recalls Aamir.

Funded by film and theatre actor Dr Shriram Lagoo, Aamir featured in this experimental movie as an actor, assistant director and a spot boy. This experience made him even more interested in filmmaking. He joined a theatre group, Avantar, where he worked backstage for two years. This enriched him as an actor.

When his Class XII results came out, Aamir announced his plan. He was not going to study further. The family relented, but Aamir was still not sure if he wanted to be a director or an actor. To understand the intricacies of film production, he joined his uncle, Nasir Hussain, on the sets of *Manzil Manzil*. At the same time, he joined the cast of film director Ketan Mehta's coming-of-age drama, *Holi*.

Mehta's film was about a day in a college campus. He wanted the feel to be organic and fancied a cast that had never acted before. The choice for the lead role in the film was between Aamir and his friend from the tennis court, Ashutosh Gowariker.

Aamir had had a recent heartbreak. He was dating a girl for a while, but then one day she said that she did not feel for him the same way. They had broken up. He was angry then and to vent his emotions, Aamir landed up on the sets with a shaven head. Shocked, Mehta asked, 'What happened to your hair?' Pat came the smart-alecky reply, 'They are no more.' Gowariker bagged the film's lead actor's role and Aamir was relegated to playing a ruffian.

But he could have never thought then, when he missed the role of the lead actor, that his first, experimental film, *Paranoia* would be the ticket to his dreams.

Affirmation as an Actor

Shabana Azmi, in the late 1970s, was working with Tahir Hussain, in the Vinod Khanna-starrer *Khoon Ki Pukaar*. She had seen *Paranoia* by then. When she met Aamir, she heaped praises on him, saying, 'Oh! You're Tahir saab's son. I must tell him you're a fantastic actor!' A shy Aamir said, 'No! You can't tell him that!' To which Azmi replied, 'Of course, I will. You are a fantastic actor, you should be acting.'

Months later, Nasir Hussain was directing *Zabardast* in Lonavla and Aamir was assisting him. Javed Akhtar had come to the hill station to work on the *Mr. India* script. Aamir was sitting in the director's room and Javed saab walked in to say hi. He looked at Aamir and asked his uncle who he was. Nasir Hussain said, 'He is Tahir's son and he is assisting me.' Javed saab instinctively blurted, 'Why is he an assistant? He should be a star!'

It was quite ironical that both Shabana Azmi and Javed Akhtar, who are a couple today, individually noticed him at different times and said the same thing about him. That started the ball rolling.

Nasir Hussain launched his next production, with a working title, *Nafrat ke Waris*. The film starred Aamir, who was jubilant. But father Tahir Hussain had seen the world. He had faced many ups and downs in his life. In fact more downs, than ups. And to add to that, he was an unsuccessful actor himself. He wondered, would the young lad have the stomach to weather it all?

3

The Outsider

lass XI, St Columba's School, Delhi. Four aghast boys of the C Gang, watched their friend go into a severe epileptic fit. The young, endearing boy with dimpled cheeks was frothing at the mouth. It continued disturbingly for a while. The alarmed teacher then urged the four friends to take the boy out of the class for immediate medical help. One of the friends requested the teacher for his leather shoe, as it was widely believed that smelling the shoe would arrest the fit. The teacher willingly obliged. The four friends left the classroom, carrying their epileptic friend on their shoulders, while the shocked teacher stayed back in class with one shoe on his feet. Out of the teacher's sight, in the corridor outside the class, the five friends broke into a jig and celebrated their successful ploy to bunk class. The credit went to the meticulous planning and deft acting skills of their friend who had played the role of the boy with the epileptic fit. This was perhaps one of the earliest affirmations of the young boy's penchant for drama.

Shah Rukh was an unusual student at St Columba's School. Remembered as a naughty child in school, he figured early in life, that his dimpled smile and sharp brain were his biggest weapons to disarm others and defend himself from getting into trouble. Once he messed up in the Chemistry lab. Before he could be pulled up for it, he went crying to the teacher. He cooked up a story of how he was treated badly at home and that that was why he was tormented and prone to making mistakes.

Another teacher, Miss Sachdeva, also fell for his sob stories. Once on the brink of punishment, he went to her, crying. With an innocent helpless look, he asked for help and told her that she was like his mother. The dimpled, innocent look of the hapless boy did the trick. Instead of doling out punishment, she consoled him and sent him away. He walked out, giggling, for having saved his skin. Seeing his shivering body from the back, his teacher thought the troubled boy was weeping inconsolably.

Brother Eric D'Souza, his middle-school headmaster, maintains, 'He was a boundary breaker. But he was also smart enough to live on the edge and not get caught.' In January 1985, when Shah Rukh passed out of St Columba's, he was given the 'Sword of Honour'. It was the school's highest award, given to a student who was an all-rounder and excelled in academics, sports and co-curricular activities. Shah Rukh, then nineteen, was the star of the year.

A Natural Entertainer

As a child, Shah Rukh didn't have a TV at home. Every Sunday evening, he used to go to his neighbour Arora saab's house, to watch movies on Doordarshan. That was the beginning of his fascination for cinema and dramatics. With his close friends from Rajendra Nagar in Delhi—Binni, Praveen, Gitthi and Vinod—he used to flock to read Inspector Vikram's action stories. Then they would write plays based on these stories and enact them. They would hoist white bed sheets and construct a temporary auditorium in Shah Rukh's balcony and tickets would be sold at ten paisa each. This was probably the beginning of acting before a packed audience that loved to watch Shah Rukh perform.

At school too, Shah Rukh's talent for mimicry had won him fans. Teachers would invite him on stage for the latest impersonations of Hindi film actors. His imitations of film-maker Raj Kapoor and Gabbar Singh, the villain from *Sholay*, were especially popular.

Shah Rukh soon started participating in Ram Leela functions that took place behind his house. He was a part of the Vanar Sena (Troupe of Monkeys). Sometimes, he used to be the filler, reciting poems to a restless audience. Often people gave the charming boy a rupee or two for his effort. Ram Leela for young Shah Rukh had a special place. It was about having a ball while monkeying around, eating bananas, shouting slogans and burning up Lanka.

His parents were always indulgent about his activities as an 'entertainer'. They would gather around a radiogram and ask him to enact the dialogues and hum the songs that played on it. Somewhere at a subtle level, his parents nurtured his latent talent. His aunt who stayed in London, gifted them a VCR and every evening, Shah Rukh pressed his mother Fatima's feet and they watched a new Hindi film unfold in front of them. Fatima was perhaps the only one who cherished Bollywood dreams for her son and was exceptionally supportive of Shah Rukh's acting.

Once Shah Rukh and Fatima visited Brother Eric, his middle-school headmaster, whom Shah Rukh looked up to. Brother Eric was known to have had the ability to channelize the energies of the boys, so that they would not get misled or lose focus in life.

Shah Rukh told him he wanted to go to Bollywood. Pat

came Brother Eric's reply, 'That's absurd. You don't know anyone there.' He then turned to Fatima to ask her what she thought of Shah Rukh's plan. Fatima's response was unexpected. With sheer firmness she said, 'If my Shah Rukh says it will happen, then it will happen.'

She was right. It happened. But unfortunately, she did not live to see it.

Early Influences

Shah Rukh was also very close to his father, Meer Taj , who was one of India's youngest freedom fighters and had even gone to jail during the freedom struggle and later had been felicitated with the Tamra Patra Award[8]. Incidentally, Shah Rukh's father had contested, but lost the elections against Maulana Abul Kalam Azad, who was the great-grandfather of Aamir Khan.

Idealist and an honest man, Meer saab started as a lawyer but did not feel morally right about the need of the trade. He ventured into business but didn't have the shrewdness to succeed. His transportation and restaurant business too shut down. During that time, freedom fighters were given a small kiosk behind Willingdon Hospital in Delhi, and he eventually started operating a tea stall from there.

Though they were financially unstable, his father turned their lives into a fun game. One such was a car-spotting game outside Kamani Auditorium, opposite Doordarshan Bhawan, Delhi. Shah Rukh and his father would eat peanuts and watch cars go by and the father would give the son a packet of peanuts and ask him to spot cars with an 'E-1' license plate. The one

---

[8]An honour given to Indian freedom fighters by the government.

KHANtastic

who spotted the most cars with these number plates would win. Shah Rukh always mentions that his father was so 'entertaining', that if he were to be left on an island with his children, he would think of a game to entertain them there too.

His father's philosophy was simple, '*Jis cheez mein dil khush ho, woh karna. Kaam karna. Nahi bhi karo toh theek hai. Jo kuch nahi karte hain, woh kamal karte hain* (Do what makes you happy. Even if you don't do anything, it's fine. Those who don't do anything, create wonders).'

However, Meer Taj too did not live long enough to see the wonders his son created. Shah Rukh lost his father to throat cancer at the early age of fifteen and even his mother to diabetes when he was twenty-five.

Life Makes the Choice

During his last days, Meer saab used to run the mess at the National School of Drama (NSD) and worked very hard to put his children through good schooling and managed it despite their financial challenges. Shah Rukh's school at that time got over at around 1.30 p.m., after which he was delegated to pick up sister Shehnaz Lalarukh from Modern School at 4 p.m. The two would then go back home together. This time gap between Shah Rukh's and Shehnaz's school getting over was spent at NSD where Shah Rukh would go to meet his father. Both Shah Rukh and his sister were very close to Meer saab. After he passed away, Shah Rukh never wrote poetry and Shehnaz plunged into depths of irreversible grief.

The time that Shah Rukh spent at NSD was precious to him. At this institution, Shah Rukh grew up amidst some of the nation's most renowned actors, Rohini Hattangadi, Raj Babbar,

Surekha Sikri and many more. They loved the charming boy with a dimple. Raj Babbar was Babbar uncle for him. Shah Rukh would watch *Suraj Ka Satvan Ghoda* sitting on director Ebrahim Alkazi's lap. The seniors taught him how to play cards. Babbar uncle, specially, taught him the game of Bluff. Having grown up at this epicentre of creativity, it was but natural for the theatre bug to bite young Shah Rukh. But Shah Rukh was in two minds, as he loved playing hockey and wanted to go forward with this sport. Unfortunately, he met with a bad injury. And life made the choice for him.

The injury halted Shah Rukh's active sporting career. He knew that though he could eventually play amateur sports, he could never be fit enough to be a professional sportsman due to the shoulder injury. Suddenly his evenings became free. Shah Rukh was getting restless, so his mother suggested theatre. He recalls, 'There was a play being performed by students of Lady Shri Ram College. The cast had eighty female students and a few roles for boys, so I was hoping against hope that something would work out for me.' But most of the casting had been done by the time Shah Rukh arrived, and he had to settle for a miniscule part of a singer in the chorus.

Soon, Shah Rukh joined the Theatre Action Group (TAG). Its founder and director, Barry John, had said, 'You should be in the movies.' He was the first person to tell Shah Rukh that. This motivated Shah Rukh immensely and his unrestrained performances stood out. In a play titled *The Incredible Vanishing*, he was required to thump another character on the back. He did this with tremendous gusto. After the first few performances, the actor requested Shah Rukh to hit him gently. In the next performance, Shah Rukh hit harder and added a few extra thumps for effect. It got a bigger laugh from

KHANtastic

the children in the audience. Even in those days, Shah Rukh had a fairly good idea of what worked with the audience. The impact was what mattered. An actor has to do whatever it takes to deliver—was his motto, and still remains so.

Shah Rukh spent five years at TAG. His personality developed and flashes of the future star shone bright in his performances in plays such as *Baghdad Ka Ghulam*.

Connecting to people with humour was always what made Shah Rukh popular since his early days. D. Ranganathan, light in-charge at TAG, remembers that once Shah Rukh and he were returning from a play and it was a day of keen vigilance by the Delhi police. At the roundabout of Taj Mahal Hotel (then Taj Mansingh), they were stopped by the police. The police asked the two boys in a strict gruff voice, 'What is inside the trunk of the car?' Prompt came a mischievous answer, 'An AK-47 and a dead body.' Then there was mayhem. Finally, the police were pacified, when the boys convinced them that it was just an irrational joke, never to be repeated again.

Lights! Camera! Action!

The first time the Badshah of Bollywood faced the camera was in 1988 for a small independently produced film called *In Which Annie Gives It Those Ones*. Directed by Pradip Krishen, now an environmentalist, and his writer-actor companion Arundhati Roy, the film was set in a Delhi architectural school in the year 1974. It was a trilingual film, as primarily the dialogues were in English but the characters did speak in Hindi and Punjabi too. The film gave a peek into college life of the 1970s, brimming with the wild abandon of free-spirited students. In Roy's words, it was 'lunatic fringe cinema' and was telecast in Doordarshan's late-night slot where few people saw it.

Krishen and Roy were players in India's art-house scene then. To make this offbeat film, Krishen approached TAG and was determined to find new actors by holding intensive workshops. In April 1988, fifteen actors, including Shah Rukh, Rituraj, Divya Seth and Benny Thomas, who later came to Bombay with Shah Rukh to help him search for his lady-love Gauri, started to participate in workshops held in a small house in the neighbourhood of Chanakyapuri. Krishen used a video camera to familiarize the actors with the nuances of the camera and to make them comfortable on-screen. To get into character, the men sprouted beards and let their hair grow.

Shah Rukh was practising for one of the lead roles. The character was called Mankind. On the last day of the workshop, to Shah Rukh's surprise, the actor who was actually supposed to play Mankind, Issac Thomas, walked in. That's when Arundhati told Shah Rukh, 'Asliwala has come, toh tum chill maro (The real Mankind has arrived. You can take it easy now).'

Shah Rukh was compensated with another role, much smaller in length and importance. So the next day, Shah Rukh, who had grown his hair and beard, walked in clean shaven and sporting short hair. When the shocked crew members asked him, 'What have you done?' he casually replied, 'The hair and beard were for Mankind. Now that I am playing another role, I have taken them off.'

This was perhaps the first and only downgrade Shah Rukh has ever experienced. In 1997, when Arundhati Roy won the Booker Prize for her remarkable novel, *The God of Small Things*, Shah Rukh Khan, who was then a star, was asked to grace the occasion. He declined. Shah Rukh had not forgotten his first rejection.

A Film-maker or a Star?

Between 1985 and 1988, Shah Rukh enrolled in Hansraj College for a bachelor's degree in economics. After graduation, he joined Jamia Millia Islamia to study for a master's degree in mass communication. He made his first earning of ₹50 as an usher in ghazal singer Pankaj Udhas's concert in Delhi. With that money, he and his friends boarded a train to Agra. It was Shah Rukh's first train journey and they wanted to visit the famous Taj Mahal. Their finances were limited. So when everyone was hungry, instead of food, they opted for a glass of pink lassi. It was not only a stomach-filling option but also a green tick on their to-do list. The experience of this sweet beverage did not end with sweet memories though. A bumble bee was suspected to have graced the drink and after having it, Shah Rukh had a bad bout of throwing up, throughout the return train journey.

Shah Rukh's life was never without drama, whether it was on stage or off it. He liked the craft of dramatic storytelling and harboured dreams of being an ad film-maker. Behind the camera was where Shah Rukh saw himself in the media world. But his mother's dream was he should become a charismatic star like Dilip Kumar.

Shah Rukh, who lost his mother early in life, emotionally shared on Rajat Sharma's *Aap Ki Adalat*, 'Today when Dilip saab says I am like his son and his wife Sairaji shows her affection by fondling my hair, I feel deeply touched. They are my surrogate family.' Saira Banu had once told him that if she had a son of her own, she would have showered her affection on him the same way she does to Shah Rukh. 'If only my mother had lived to see this affection,' Shah Rukh laments.

4

Aamir: *Papa Kehte Hain Bada Naam Karega*

A young boy from a film family, who chose films over tennis, rebelling quietly against his family's wish of a stable profession, sat with a poker face watching the song recording of the then rising playback singer, Alka Yagnik. It was the recording of the song 'Gazab ka hai din' for the film *Qayamat Se Qayamat Tak*.

Alka noticed this young boy sitting quietly, staring at her. Initially, she ignored him and carried on with her rehearsals. But when the recording started, she was uncomfortable. The boy's gaze was constant and he wasn't even blinking an eyelid. Alka was ticked off and threw the boy out of the room. Much after the recording was done, the director of the film, Mansoor Khan, introduced Alka to the actor who was debuting as the lead in the film. It was none other than the poker-faced boy who was staring at her, Aamir Khan. Alka was visibly embarrassed and did not know what to say then to Mansoor and Aamir. Aamir however, even today, does not let go of a chance to pull her leg, reminding her of that incident. Alka still gets uncomfortable and embarrassed remembering it.

The Making of a Hysteria

The title of the film—*Nafrat Ke Waris*—seemed apt at that point of time. But as days passed, Nasir Hussain, the producer of the film, wasn't keen on this title. He thought it was negative and gory in nature. He expressed his displeasure to son Mansoor, daughter Nuzhat and Aamir. *Daraar* became the next working title for the film, but that too didn't last for long. One day, Hussain called the trio and told them that he had come up with an apt name, *Qayamat Se Qayamat Tak*. Everyone was dumbfounded and thought it was too long and an overdramatic title. An unsure Mansoor shared the title with lyricist Majrooh Sultanpuri, who the family looked up to. Sultanpuri too loved it, and thus *Nafrat Ke Waris* became *Qayamat Se Qayamat Tak*.

Initially, Hussain himself was to direct the film and not Mansoor. But before the film could take off, he fell ill and had to undergo a bypass surgery in the United States. Doctors instructed him not to take on the stress of directing a full-fledged film and Hussain requested his son to take over the responsibility. Mansoor, a foreign-returned techie, who had dropped out of studies from renowned institutes such as Cornell University and Massachusetts Institute of Technology (MIT), was then working on a film called *Jo Jeeta Wohi Sikandar*.

When Hussain made him listen to his breezy Romeo-Juliet love story, with an essence of feuding thakurs as its backdrop, Mansoor's first question to his father was, 'What is a thakur?' Mansoor was completely oblivious of the concept of thakurs fighting for respect and revenge.

Mansoor finally agreed to make the film, but he made it clear to his father that he would do so on his own terms, without any interference. The first step would be to audition the lead hero, his cousin, Aamir, even though Hussain had already cast him. Hussain had announced on the sets of his last film that Aamir was to be the hero of the film. Aamir had the good looks, and the filmmaking knowledge after having assisted his uncle, but that clearly wasn't enough for Mansoor. They were brothers, had grown up together, but Mansoor had to be sure that Aamir had it in him to act.

Meanwhile, Aamir was dedicatedly training for the film. He had joined Roshan Taneja's acting classes and was even practising stunts at Juhu beach. One day, when he hurt his back doing stunts, Hussain who got to know about this, told him to stop right away. 'You are going to be an actor, not a stuntman,' thundered the uncle.

Aamir auditioned for Mansoor and thankfully, for all concerned, Mansoor was convinced that Aamir was good to be Romeo, the Raj of *Qayamat Se Qayamat Tak*. Now what remained was to put together a crew of Mansoor's choice and cast the perfect Juliet, as Rashmi.

The screen test was held in the backyard of Hussain's house. Two or three girls had been called for the audition and one of them, Alisha Chinoy (later Alisha Chinai), didn't even land up for the screen test. Such was the excitement surrounding the film! Juhi Chawla, an upcoming model and Miss India 1984 winner, was asked to enact a scene from the film, *Yaadon Ki Baaraat*. Not confident at all, she approached none other than Aamir, who was there at the audition, to help her prepare and he obliged. Aamir taught Juhi how to do the scene and the audition was held under a tree in the garden of Hussain's bungalow. Luckily for Juhi, she passed with flying colours.

Even the film's supporting cast—Alok Nath, Dalip Tahil and Reema Lagoo—was relatively new. It's a different story that Nath and Lagoo would, in the future, go on to become household names with a film which would introduce another romantic hero into the film world, eighteen months later.

With fairly new faces playing pivotal roles, the stalwarts of the industry doubted its success. In those days, the reaction was predictable. '*Ladka naya hai, music directors naye hai, director naya hai—kaise chalegi picture?* (The boy is new, the music directors are new, the director is new—how will the film work?)'. In fact, when the team was shooting in Mount Abu, Tahil, who played Aamir's father in the film, was the only one signing autographs. He was the star on the sets of *Qayamat Se Qayamat Tak* till young Aamir strummed his guitar and sang 'Papa kehte hain bada naam karega' to set cinema screens on fire on a Friday of 1988.

Aamir's introduction song in *Qayamat Se Qayamat Tak*, 'Papa kehte hai bada naam karega', still remains a memorable part of the film. As does the scene where Aamir is jogging with the rising sun in the background. In that particular scene, Juhi was seen clicking pictures of the beautiful sunrise when she noticed Aamir, in silhouette, running towards her. Seldom has an actor looked so heroic as he strode forth with the striking orange fireball behind him. However, Aamir's introduction/entry scene in the film was not planned in the way it actually took place on screen. He was initially supposed to be working on his typewriter, when a snake slithers up to him. Aamir was to pet the snake and only then it would be apparent that he was a pet lover, and that the snake was his pet. Nasir Hussain hated the idea, and threw it out of the window. It was replaced with the iconic entry that brought the theatres down. Kiran Deohans, the cinematographer, remembers that while taking a close shot, he could not help noticing how endearing Aamir

Sanjukta Nandy

looked with a warm, golden light on his hair, enhancing his charm that would rock a million hearts.

Unlike most actors, Aamir was deeply involved in the making of the film. It was his direction and production background and his meticulous preparations that were a great help on the sets. But even he wasn't prepared for what awaited them on the first outdoor schedule of the film.

The schedule was a forty-day shoot in Ooty. Aamir remembers vividly that there was a scene where Juhi and he are lost in the jungle at night. Then they meet and catch some sleep. But when Aamir wakes up in the morning, she isn't there anymore, as she has gone to the river to get water. Aamir's first shot was the one where he wakes up to find that she wasn't there. The shot was ready but after a couple of takes, the fog took over and the shoot was stalled. Everyone waited patiently for the fog to lift so that they could resume work, but the weather gods were adamant and they had to pack up. The first day of outdoor being a washout, Aamir prayed that this was not a bad omen setting a precedent for the future.

Shooting every scene for Aamir was hell. He recalls, 'Not just the dramatic ones, even the romantic scenes didn't come easy. To look deep into a girl's eyes and try to convince myself that you're madly in love with her, when she's just a stranger you've met some months back, was tough.'

While shooting the song 'Gazab ka hai din', the fog and rain once again played spoilsport and kept a crew of over fifty people waiting. This continued for a couple of days when the unit would reach the location but was unable to shoot because of lack of light. The crew eventually started playing cricket, to keep their morale high.

One day while shooting, Deohans, looking into the lens,

found that the mountain had turned upside down. It was actually not the mountain but the camera that had turned around. It had fallen off the slippery trolley and the lens was broken. To add to their woes, the set, built near the temple on a hill, that was to be Aamir and Juhi's house, was razed to the ground by the October rains. It had to be rebuilt. The budget was predetermined. It was a movie with a new crew and cast. The odds were steep and Aamir started to wonder whether this film was going to be the biggest mistake of his life.

Yet Aamir took all this as a challenge, pioneering his energy and kept the smile on everyone's face. The camaraderie between Aamir and Mansoor was inspiring for the whole team. It was like they knew what was happening in each other's heads. In the scene where Aamir secretly comes to meet Juhi, Mansoor was not fully satisfied with Aamir's take. He was wondering if Aamir was up to give another take. Before he could even come up with this suggestion and discuss it, Aamir asked for another take. Such was the bond between the brothers.

In the climax scene, after Juhi was shot, Aamir was to scream out 'Rashmi, Rashmi' and then stab himself. Aamir was charged up and Mansoor shouted 'Action'. Aamir ran to Rashmi (Juhi) and almost at the end of a perfect take, he screamed 'Juhi, Juhi'. Mansoor had to cut the scene, leaving Aamir wondering why Mansoor had abruptly ended a take that was going so well. Finally, Aamir realized his mistake and figured that he was so engrossed that the boundary between fiction and reality had blurred.

Mansoor Khan was reportedly mortified when he saw the complete film for the first time at a trial kept for the inner circle. 'I was cringing…*kya bakwas hai, yaar*! (What nonsense!)' recalls Mansoor. He remembers coming out of the screening having noticed what he considered glaring mistakes, while his father had a bounce of victory in his step.

The 1980's Most Promising Find

Nasir Hussain was all charged up for the next inevitable step. The release of the film. There were numerous trials for buyers from all over India. After every screening, the reactions were disappointing—some found the music weak, some didn't like the title, but almost every single one of them objected to the tragic ending. They loved the film but unanimously felt that it had a huge margin of risk with newcomers and a tragic ending. They were ready to pick up the film but only with a positive ending.

Unfortunately for Hussain, Mansoor was adamant that he would not associate with the film if the end was changed. Even though the positive ending was shot, Mansoor was not even ready to edit it. The father would try to convince the son that he should reconsider his decision, but Nuzhat and Aamir would defend Mansoor's defiance. Hussain was caught in a crossfire between the distributors and his family. Selling the film was an uphill task and it took the veteran producer almost a year to close all territories.

When it was time to publicize the film, a unique marketing campaign was devised by Mansoor, Nuzhat and Aamir. A series of three large hoardings went up across Bombay.

The first hoarding featured a full-length image of Aamir, his back to the camera, with a caption that read, 'Who is Aamir Khan?' After a week, the second billboard came up with Aamir's image. It read, 'Ask the Girls Next Door.' Finally, a week later, the last billboard featured a third line that read,

'See him in *Qayamat Se Qayamat Tak*.'

Aamir, along with Raj Zutshi, his co-star and friend who married cousin Nuzhat, personally glued posters of the film on every rickshaw he could find in Bombay. Juhi, too, requested a few taxi drivers to put up stickers of the film, featuring Aamir and herself. When they asked her, '*Kaun hai yeh dono*? (Who are these two?)', she shyly admitted that it was she in the film.

Most producers then would avoid a release during Ramzan, but Hussain decided to release it right then, as he was sure this would give the film an uninterrupted run in the theatres.

The night before the release, Aamir needed moral support and stayed over at his close friend, director Satyajit Bhatkal's house. Aamir had once told Bhatkal that if films didn't work out for him, he would become a flight purser[9]. But easier said than done. Aamir was so tense for the film to work that he stayed awake all night.

D-Day arrived and Aamir bought tickets for the noon show by himself and arrived at Bandra's Gaiety-Galaxy theatre (now known as G7), accompanied by a large group of friends and family. 'We could hear audible gasps and, by the end of the film, the whole theatre was crying,' recalls Aamir. Once the lights came on and an emotional Aamir made his way out, he heard people saying, '*Arre yaar, yeh toh abhi picture mein tha. Yeh toh apna hero hai!* (This is the guy who was in the film. He is our hero!).'

Aamir had arrived with a bang. *Qayamat Se Qayamat Tak* went on to become a phenomenon and a landmark in Bollywood history. Interestingly, it started the abbreviation culture or the shortened phrase for long titles. Later *Maine*

---

[9]Chief flight attendant in an airline.

Sanjukta Nandy

Pyar Kiya became *MPK*, *Dilwale Dulhania Le Jayenge* was popular as *DDLJ* while *Hum Aapke Hain Koun..!* was *HAHK*. This trend had to thank *QSQT* (*Qayamat Se Qayamat Tak*) for it.

The Illustrated Weekly of India described the impact of this phenomenon:

> Not since Bobby had a love story struck pay dirt at the box-office in such a big way... Nothing was close to the hysteria unleashed by *Qayamat Se Qayamat Tak*. It swept the nation, spawned street-savvy imitators, had the masses charmed with its hero and mesmerised by its music. Suddenly, after years, filmdom had produced a star, who seemed poised to take a permanent position in the pantheon of the greats.[10]

Filmfare wrote: 'Aamir Khan is perhaps the most promising find of the '80s. A boy of small build with no affectations and no mannerisms.' This was the 'Aamir-impact' that had swept the nation off its feet.

Aamir, who had received a remuneration of ₹11,000 for the film and used public transport, now started getting recognized and mobbed by his fans. At the height of the Aamir hysteria, at *Qayamat Se Qayamat Tak's* hundred-day celebrations in Calcutta (now Kolkata), frenzied fans reportedly almost tore off Aamir's clothes.

The film went on to win the National Award for Best Popular Film Providing Wholesome Entertainment in the 36th National Film Award and Aamir received a special mention in

---

[10]Christina Daniels, *I'll Do It My Way: The Incredible Journey of Aamir Khan*, Om Books International, 2012

the ceremony in 1989. It also swept the 34th Filmfare Awards where Aamir stirred the hearts of the audience, by lip-syncing to 'Papa kehte hain bada naam karega...' and picked up the Best Male Debut Award for the 1988 release.

After a successful era of the Angry Young Man, the audience had been given a dose of innocence and romance. It started a trend of 'the chocolate lover boy'. The audience were just at the beginning of an insatiable appetite for youthful freshness. Aamir now held centre stage, but little did he know then that the birth of another heartthrob was just round-the-corner.

Come December 1989, and a 'Prem' would take the nation by storm.

Salman: *Maine Pyar Kiya*

*I*t was a cool morning of December 1989, when a young boy rode pillion on his friend's bike as they headed for a theatre in South Bombay to see the first screening of a new film. Even though he was not a morning person, he sat wide awake with excitement. It was his own debut as the film's lead and he was keen to know his fate. His posters were all over the country and he was hoping that people would recognize him. As he entered the theatre, his heart started to palpitate with anticipation. Unfortunately, no one even looked at him. Not then.

The boy had featured in a couple of advertisements and was in a miniscule role in a film, *Biwi Ho To Aisi*, that had released in August the previous year but had sunk without a trace. This, his second feature, was a movie with a new star cast, a new director and a production house known for its small-budget family films only.

Interval announced the pulse of the film and after 195 minutes of the first show of *Maine Pyar Kiya*, the verdict was out. When the twenty-four-year-old headed for the next theatre, he had a huge crowd running behind their bike, furiously chasing him. A new craze—Salman Khan, alias Prem—was born.

At Satyam Theatre, Worli, however, when Salman met director David Dhawan, the reaction was different. Dhawan had come there to see the response to his big-budget release, *Aag Ka Gola*, which had released on the same day. Concern was writ all over Dhawan's face. Not for himself, but for Salman. What was going to be the fate of Salim Khan's son? How would *Maine Pyar Kiya* stand up to the Goliath of a film he had made?

But Salman had seen the reaction of the previous audience, so he held on to his nerves. Once the doors of Satyam opened at interval, Dhawan's expression had changed. He knew Salim Khan's son had arrived.

Salman became an overnight sensation. *Maine Pyar Kiya* went on to become the biggest grosser of the year. The date—29 December 1989—ended up changing many lives, but not without their having lived through its fair share of agony and insecurity.

In the late 1980s, Rajshri Productions was going through a lean phase. Action films were the flavour of the season. The comfort of the VCR and home viewing had started eating into the numbers of theatre-goers. To combat these changes, they decided to make a musical love story with extraordinary music. Sooraj, the third generation of the Barjatyas, was chosen to write and direct the film.

Average film budgets in those days were of about ₹70–80 lakh and the last film the Barjatyas had made, had a budget of nearly ₹40 lakh. But the Barjatyas wanted to up their game and this film was made with a whopping ₹1-crore budget. Even Lata Mangeshkar stepped in and rendered the songs with her mellifluous voice. The launched film turned into a grand opus. It also had a small release in eighteen theatres with only eighteen prints. The stakes were extremely high and it was make-or-break time.

It all began with Sooraj Barjatya's father, Raj Kumar Barjatya, asking him to write a love story. He wrote it in English and then his father asked him to translate it in Hindi. After reading the script, the family unanimously decided that it should be made with a new boy and a new girl. The hunt began, to search for Prem and Suman.

Various actors came into the fray. Deepak Tijori was considered. It did not happen. Deep Raj Rana auditioned. He was rejected. Piyush Mishra was considered. He rejected it. Mohnish Bahl auditioned for it. He was given the villain's role instead. Finally, Vindoo Dara Singh was chosen and the film went on the floors. However, after just one day of shooting, for unknown reasons, Vindoo was out of the film and the search for the hero began once again.

Faraaz Khan, the son of actor Yusuf Khan (popular for the role of Zebisko in *Amar Akbar Anthony*), was finalized. But he fell seriously ill with jaundice. Fate played a cruel game with Faraaz and he had to opt out due to health issues.

Simultaneously, Sooraj was holding auditions for the role of Suman for which a girl named Shabana Dutt had auditioned. Sooraj remembers that while she was screen testing, she recommended a certain Salman Khan with whom she had worked in a footwear advertisement. Till date, Salman credits her for making him the 'Prem' that the world is fond of. Incidentally her whereabouts are unknown and neither Salman nor Sooraj has been able to trace her, despite their best efforts.

Meeting the Barjatyas

Apart from Shabana Dutt, three other people had recommended Salman to the Barjatyas. Salim Khan's assistant writer knew

Guptaji, the manager at Rajshri Productions. He had put in a strong word along with Honey Irani, who went on to become a well-known writer. They said, '*Dekho yeh ladka kuch nahi kar raha hai. Agar aapke paas kuch role ho, toh de do usko* (This boy isn't doing much. If you have a role, please give it to him).' During that period, another writer had come to Salman to narrate a script that the latter had politely declined. This writer was accompanied by another writer-friend, who understood Salman's sensibilities and recommended him to the Barjatyas, saying, '*Ek ladka aaya tha... Salim Khan ka beta. Sensible ladka hai. Toh usko try karo* (A boy had come. Salim Khan's son. He is sensible. So try him out).' The ripple effect of all these recommendations landed Salman at the Rajshri Productions office.

When Salman walked into Sooraj's cabin for the first time, the initial thought that crossed the producer-director's mind was that he was very small to look at. But when Salman showed his photographs, Sooraj realized that this boy had a special relationship with the lens. The camera loved him.

Sooraj then narrated the script of the film to Salman. As the story unfolded, Salman could not visualize other actors like Jackie Shroff, Sanjay Dutt, Sunny Deol or Kumar Gaurav, but only himself playing the character of Prem. Salman could hear the words in his head, '*Isko jaane mat do bhai, yeh tumhari life banayega.* (Don't let this go. This will make your career).' As soon as the narration was over, Salman said, 'Sooraj, it's superb, man! We'll do a great film together.' 'But, Salman, I have not signed you yet,' Sooraj was quick to respond.

Sooraj then revealed that there were other choices to be considered for the lead role. Salman did not bat an eyelid and immediately gave him a list of friends' names who were struggling actors. Samsher, Vishal Verma, Mustafa, Hanu Tiwary Gujral, Deepak Malhotra—and the list went on and on. Sooraj was shocked and asked Salman why he was doing this and further diminishing his own chances. Salman was clear. If he didn't get the film, he would be happy if someone from his gang of friends got it. Sooraj, an emotional person, had never met anyone so large-hearted. Impressed, he told Salman that he had crossed over from the first round into the audition round.

Just a week before his birthday in December, Salman was to audition. But on that very day, he suddenly came down with a severe sinus attack. He could not say his dialogues properly. Even his dance steps went haywire, although he had prepared well. He immediately called his friend-choreographer Farah Khan for a practice session and told her she would have to accompany him to the audition for moral support.

Farah arrived to help her friend along with Chow Mow, her dancing partner, in tow. The premise for the class was set at Juhu Beach and Salman wanted to learn the front somersault in half an hour. In the first three attempts, Salman fell flat on his face, but in the fourth attempt, he got it right.

Happily, well prepared, the duo left for the audition in Salman's Fiat. At a bungalow in Worli, where the test shoot was held, Salman got carried away and started to do a freestyle dance. This left Farah aghast and she switched sides. She told Sooraj that as it was his first film, he should reconsider his choices and stomped out of the audition.

The audition continued. The gates were open and a dishevelled young lover ran into the bungalow as his loosely worn shirt flew in the air and he stood facing the camera. The background played the famous track of 'Dil deewana bin sajna ke mane na'. The boy looked straight into the camera and held up a bunch of tattered notes.

After that, Salman did some shots with the guitar on, 'Oh Hansini.' Sooraj showed it to Charu and Chanda, his cousin and sister, who approved.

Salman was sure he had cracked it, but for months after that he did not get a call. Clearly, Sooraj wasn't impressed. It was all over. Four months passed. Salman was back to struggling for work.

During this time, Salman went for each and every audition that he got to know of. A new producer, Suresh Bhagat, was making a film, *Biwi Ho To Aisi* and J.K. Bihari, the production manager of K.C. Bokadia, a successful producer and director of the 1980s, was directing it. It was the remake of a Pakistani film and had an ensemble star cast. They were looking for a boy to play the role of Vicky Bhandari, the younger brother of the lead, Suraj Bhandari, a character to be enacted by Farooq Sheikh.

When Salman walked into a garage in Khar, Mumbai, for the audition, he was immediately selected. The scenario was very different from the *Maine Pyar Kiya* audition. Later, Bihari told him that no one had wanted to play this role. In desperation, the frustrated crew had decided that whoever walked in next would be cast for this character. It was Salman's destiny that he was next. He bagged the role, only to realize that this choice might have cost him the role of Prem in *Maine Pyar Kiya*. Sooraj hadn't given up the thought of casting Salman, but did after hearing that he had signed up for *Biwi Ho To Aisi*. He did not want to cast a boy who had been chosen to do a supporting role in a small film.

Sooraj felt he should inform Salman about his decision.

Salman then was shooting for *Biwi Ho To Aisi* in Bombay and as soon as Salman saw Sooraj walk in, he hugged him. Sooraj broke the news that Salman was not the chosen one for Prem.

This did not deter Salman. He immediately suggested another set of names for the role. Salman used to search for roles in films carrying three portfolios with him. His own, Suniel Shetty's, whom he lovingly calls Anna till date, and another actor-friend, Sunny's portfolio. And of course, all his other actor-friends were also on his recommendation list. Sooraj was so stunned at this boy's nature that he went back to office and declared to his team, '*Agar koi hero banega, toh yehi banega* (If there is anyone who will play the hero, it is he).'

Salman's journey, to be synonymous with Prem, began, but another obstacle cropped up. The Barjatyas soon discovered that Suresh Bhagat had a multiple film contract with Salman. They went to meet him, requesting him to let Salman off and Bhagat obliged. Salman had cooperated well with Bhagat and had even worn his own clothes for the film and his good deed paid off. The young Salman, who was known to spend his evenings having a good time with his friends and doing nothing at a small park near an old bungalow in Bandra, the one the world today knows as Shah Rukh's Mannat, was to be the lead of one of the biggest-budget films of the year.

The New Craze

On the first day of the shoot, the pressure was too much for Sooraj to handle. Salman was a new actor. Bhagyashree, the female lead was new. Raamlaxman, the music director, was a debutant. Sooraj, himself, was helming his first feature and the Barjatyas had put the family's reputation and big money on this venture. The first scene was shot at Natraj Studios. It was raining heavily and as the huge set waged the rains, Sooraj feared they had begun the shoot on the wrong foot. People said this was just like the rain and fog fiasco that happened on Aamir's *Qayamat Se Qayamat Tak* set in Ooty. 'What would happen to our future? Where would this movie go?' wondered Sooraj. Then he broke down and wept like a baby. And Salman cried along with him.

Later, as the film progressed, this became regular. After the first schedule was completed, the set was dismantled and an emotional Sooraj cried. They built another set and Sooraj cried again. They built the third and yet again, Sooraj cried. They finished shooting and Sooraj cried once again. And whenever Sooraj cried, Salman, equally overwhelmed, cried with him. The two were at the beginning of their careers, carrying a huge responsibility on their novice shoulders. Huge money and their fate depended on *Maine Pyar Kiya* and after every schedule, they got closer to the completion and were swamped with such emotional outbursts. It was only after Sooraj's grandfather, Tarachand Barjatya, saw the rushes and advised him to keep it going, did the team feel they were on the right track.

After the first copy of the film went to the experienced sound engineer, Sooraj and Salman were in for a rude shock. The engineer recommended that Salman's voice be dubbed. Sooraj was completely against it. So, they decided to re-dub all of Salman's dialogues in the afternoon, when his voice sounded the best.

The rest, as they say, is history.

When released on 29 December 1989, the masses loved *Maine Pyar Kiya,* and it earned several records to its credit. The film received twelve Filmfare Award nominations in 1990 and won six of them—Best Film, Best Male Debut, Lux New Face of the Year, Best Music, Best Male Playback Singer and Best Lyricist. The film wrote a new success story when it was dubbed in English as *When Love Calls*. The dubbed version was the biggest hit in the Caribbean market in Guyana and also dominated the box office in Trinidad and Tobago. Later, the film was dubbed as *Te Amo* in Spanish.

Salman rapidly emerged as the new poster boy of young India. *Maharashtra Herald* wrote about the arrival of India's newest youth icon, 'Salman fit right into the niche that Aamir had carved.' The young crowd was hungry. They had been given a bite of the romantic pie with *Qayamat Se Qayamat Tak*, and *Maine Pyar Kiya* gave them a bigger bite of the pie. Comparisons started between Aamir and Salman and in May 1990, *Filmfare* put Salman on the cover and declared him 'The New Craze'.

But shockingly, even after a year of the film's success, Salman had not received any new film offers. Salim Khan made a phone call to his producer-friend's office to ask him for a favour. The friend simply had to announce in the trade papers that he had signed Salman. This was expected to help Salman get some offers. The producer-friend had once produced Salim Khan's biggest film ever, *Sholay*. His name was G.P. Sippy.

Sippy not only announced a film with Salman, but eventually made it. As soon as this film was announced, Salman had offers pouring in. The film, *Patthar Ke Phool*, when released, was another blockbuster.

Incidentally, it was G.P. Sippy who also signed another newcomer for his next film. The film was *Raju Ban Gaya Gentleman* and the newcomer was the 'Fauji' boy, Shah Rukh Khan.

6

Shah Rukh as Fauji

'*Abhi!... Abhimanyu!... Fauji!.*'

It was the streets of Delhi that first shouted out recognition to Shah Rukh Khan.

It was on 18 January 1989, a Wednesday evening, when the first episode of the television series *Fauji*, directed by Colonel Raj Kapoor, was aired on DD National. The episode took off with Abhimanyu Rai (fondly mentioned as Abhi) walking in with his friend, Peter, to the Commando Training Unit. By the end of its runtime of twenty-four minutes, Abhimanyu Rai with his deep dimples, unruly hair, brown eyes and live-wire intensity had walked straight into the hearts of Indian TV viewers.

'I am known as the man who made *Fauji* and therefore, by default, made Shah Rukh Khan. I've been an actor. I've fought three wars. But all that anybody seems to remember is that I launched Shah Rukh,' lamented Colonel Kapoor, decades later. Such is the magic of Shah Rukh Khan.

Shah Rukh, however, credits his success to having been at the right place, at the right time and with the right people. He believes he has simply been lucky, which bears out given the serendipitous manner in which he learnt of the role. Later, after an enduring performance in a tough audition, he bagged only a small part but then went on to play the lead role of Abhimanyu Rai in *Fauji*.

It all begun when Shah Rukh and his mother, Fatima, were house-hunting in Delhi. Colonel Kapoor's son-in-law, Kamal, was into real estate and was showing Fatima some houses. Shah Rukh's mother mentioned to him that her son had gone for theatre rehearsals with Barry John and so they would decide on the property once he was back.

Kamal promptly said, 'My father-in-law is directing and producing a television serial. Why don't you ask your son to meet him?' Shah Rukh then lived in Gautam Nagar, which was near the colonel's office. So off he went to meet the colonel. When the army man met him for the very first time, he asked Shah Rukh, 'You want to play the role of a commando?' Shah Rukh nodded, 'Yes, sir, I will do the role very well.' Shah Rukh had always wanted to join the army, but his mother and aunts were not upbeat about it. He was the family's only boy child and they did not want to send him away and 'risk it all'. *Fauji* was an opportunity to live that dream.

Along with the other boys who had come for the audition, the colonel took him out for a run. It was an endurance test. The ex-army man and director of the series had strongly resolved that as the boys were going to be enacting the lives of commandoes, they needed to be fit to look the part. Most of the boys gave up and left midway but not Shah Rukh. He stayed back and bagged a part.

Originally, it was a small part. He had to play a soldier who makes a mistake and is punished. His senior was to command him to go up to a tree and count the number of crows. Shah Rukh was to run up and come back saying, *'Char kauwe hain* (There are four crows).'* To this the senior was to say, *'Thik hai. Jawan savdhan* (Fine. Attention, soldier).'*

Shah Rukh was initially hesitant, thinking how he would

tell his mother that his contribution to the serial was that of counting crows. Fortunately, he didn't land up doing the scene. The reason was the colonel's son, Bobby.

Milin Kapoor, alias Bobby, was the cinematographer for the series and was to play the lead role. He decided that being both in front and behind the camera, was not possible for him. Bobby chose to stay behind the camera and Shah Rukh replaced him in the forefront. Abhimanyu Rai (supposedly based on the exploits of Lieutenant Colonel Sanjoy Bannerji of the Bombay Sappers, the Indian Army) was the stroke of luck that marked Shah Rukh's big moment under the spotlight.

Fauji Faux Pas

The *Fauji* team was young. It was a lot of work, fused with a lot of fun. Colonel used to be very strict about the code of conduct when his *Fauji* boys were to meet the real soldiers. Young actors were warned not to talk much to the soldiers and reveal their ignorance about the army. Once when the actors were interacting with real commandoes, one actor pointed at a black cat's pouch and asked what was inside. 'Magazines' came the curt reply from a commando. Mistaking the armoury 'magazines' to be periodicals, the boy remarked, 'Aha! They are to be read during free time.' The entire bunch of boys was extremely embarrassed and did not know where to hide their faces.

Shah Rukh was hard-working, enthusiastic and immersed in his character, so much so that he was ready to take risks. There was a scene in which the enemy jeep was to turn around the corner and he was to dive sharply into the hedge. Colonel was all prepared to use a body double. But Shah Rukh had other plans. He told the colonel that he would like to do the stunt himself. Colonel was not sure, but Shah Rukh was persuasive. Lights-camera-action, and he took a searing dive and in a single somersault went over the hedge. When the panicked Colonel shouted 'Cut', he was sure he would find his hero with a broken neck. To his surprise, a grinning Shah Rukh came out, dimples intact.

Although *Fauji* was telecast first, the first serial that Shah Rukh acted in was *Dil Dariya* by Lekh Tandon. Tandon was an established film-maker who had directed Rajshri Productions' *Dulhan Wahi Jo Piya Man Bhaaye*. When approached by young Shah Rukh for a role, Tandon found his nature to be unique. He recalled, 'Shah Rukh was so in-the-moment, respectful, charming and had a lopsided smile that could mesmerize anyone in front of him.' Tandon told Shah Rukh that if he agreed to have a haircut, he would have a role for him. Shah Rukh, who was very possessive about his hair, first made Tandon commit to the role and then took the plunge.

Tandon and Shah Rukh again teamed up for another serial, *Doosra Keval*. Tandon's observation about Shah Rukh's capacity to hold an audience captive proved clairvoyant. Years later, on Shah Rukh's request, Tandon played his grandfather in the film *Chennai Express*. He was just happy working with Shah Rukh and never claimed any fees. But the King Khan sent him a token of ₹11 lakh.

Forerunner on the TV Map

The 'Fauji''s fizzy, zestful charm was not missed by the then Brahma-Vishnu-Mahesh, of Indian television. Kundan Shah, Saeed and Aziz Mirza, who were reverentially referred to as the

Holy Trinity for their cult work, called Shah Rukh to Bombay. He bid adieu to his awestruck TAG friends in Delhi and left for Bombay. Good times had begun. However, the reception he received at the Bombay airport was another story.

He arrived in Bombay on an early morning Air India flight and found that no one from the production company was there to receive him. Roy Tellis, the assistant who was supposed to fetch Shah Rukh, had overslept. Shah Rukh panicked and thought he would call his mother and tell her that he was a victim of a shameful hoax. No one was coming for him.

Alone in an unfamiliar city, he had company from a group of Haj pilgrims waiting for their flight to the Gulf. The women in their burkhas had begun to murmur. They noticed that the effervescent boy from *Fauji* was in distress. As they went past him, they gently promised to remember him in their prayers at their pilgrimage. They quietly assured him that one day he would be a famous star.

Shah Rukh was finally able to call a friend who drove him to the Mirza brothers' and Kundan Shah's Iskra office, the production company that had asked Shah Rukh to come down to Bombay. Soon enough, Aziz Mirza saw a young boy in his office asking him for permission to make a phone call. As he watched the boy dial a number, he noticed there was something unusually interesting about him. Shah Rukh reminded Mirza of his son, Haroon, and he had an undeniably endearing energy. Mirza knew this was a star in the making.

Shah Rukh was hired to act in two serials that the company was making and thus he started living on the office couch. Even in those days, Shah Rukh liked to sleep until late. But as the office opened at 9 a.m., the young Khan would have to be up early. He was greeted with tea and sumptuous Gujarati food.

Haroon became his best friend while Mirza's wife, Nirmala, mothered him with love and care. Shah Rukh found both, work and a surrogate family, in Bombay. He often acknowledged them later, saying they were not just film-makers, they were life-makers.

In a short time, Shah Rukh was acting in three serials for Iskra—*Umeed*, *Wagle Ki Duniya* and *Circus*. Pocketing the lead for *Circus* was just like *Fauji*, a golden stroke of luck. The in-house lead actor, Pavan Malhotra, had been offered the lead in a film called *Bagh Bahadur* and he could not adjust shooting schedules. So Shah Rukh stepped into his shoes. He was to play Shekharan, the circus owner's son, who returns from his foreign studies only to get sucked into the intrigue of his family circus business. Adhering to the essence of the series, the cast and crew too travelled like a family with the real-life Apollo Circus. Over a period of three months, they toured small towns and villages of Goa and Maharashtra. Shah Rukh's co-stars in *Circus* were Renuka Shahane and Ashutosh Gowariker—the actor who bagged the role of the hero from right under a then bald Aamir's nose in the film *Holi*.

Shahane remembers that during the course of the shoot, when the team travelled in buses to places like Pune, Satara, Ratnagiri and Goa, the game of Antakshari was the icebreaker and throughout the journey, the team sang songs. Shah Rukh was really good at it. Not only that, he went out of his way to make Shahane, who was shy and travelling for the first time all by herself, comfortable. During a shoot at Ratnagiri, more than 20,000 people had come to see Shah Rukh shoot. He was a star, yet a down-to-earth team player, who would at times sit and eat with the spot boys too.

Even Vinita Malik, who played Shah Rukh's mother in

Doosra Keval, fondly remembers him as a bolt of boundless energy and enthusiasm. During the long hours of shoot, which sometimes spilled to more than forty-eight hours, Shah Rukh would never tire. His infectious energy motivated and kept the entire unit going. The shoot used to be in a village where the unit bonded over food, songs and merriment. Shah Rukh never forgot the friends he made and Malik still believes that it was Shah Rukh who had years later recommended her to Mani Ratnam for *Dil Se*. Not only that, he helped her to understand the working pattern of the film-maker and supported her to play his mother in the film.

Aziz Mirza had once said, 'Shah Rukh spoils you as a director. The amount of energy he can thrust into a role, is phenomenal. He is pure intense energy.' It was true. Working long hours was his stimulant. Those days, two units were at work to meet the deadline of *Circus*. Shah Rukh was practically in every scene, so sometimes he would work in the mornings with Mirza and work night shifts at Kundan Shah's shoot. There were instances when he did not get time even to have a bath and would just wet his hair, apply a generous amount of deodorant and was ready to seize the day. Another thing that kept him going were cigarettes and the newly introduced Pepsi.

Shah Rukh was gaining tremendous popularity with his work. His mother's dream of seeing him as a coveted star was on the rise and he wanted to share it with her. He was keen to show her his performance in *Circus*, but her diabetic health was deteriorating rapidly and she was admitted to Batra Hospital, Delhi, in 1991, fighting multiple organ failure. Shah Rukh had hooked-up a television set in her room to show her some episodes, but she was delirious and could not comprehend much. Blood poisoning or septicaemia soon took over and she slipped into a coma.

Shah Rukh was at her bedside. He knew it was time to let her go. But he was not ready. He wanted to keep God busy, listening to his prayers and not having the time to take his mother away. Over and over again, in the hospital parking lot, he prayed alone: *'Nasrun minal lahe wah fatahun kareeb',* a sportsman's prayer that meant, God give me the strength to win.[11] Soon his mother was barely breathing. He now tried the last ace up his sleeve.

Shah Rukh strongly believed that a person only left the body when they were fully satisfied. He kept telling her things that would make her angry, like he will not study, not work and not look after his sister. He kept an eye on the medical monitor that spiked up the irregular numbers. But soon the life monitor beeped in straight lines. Today, Shah Rukh feels she must have known he was lying. 'God knows better and mother knows best,' he sighs.

The loss of his mother drove Shah Rukh into despair. Every bit of Delhi and his home reminded him of her. He decided to stay on in Bombay. He moved into his friend Vivek Vaswani's Cuffe Parade house and then to one of Aziz Mirza's vacant apartments. Nirmala, Mirza's wife, had become his surrogate mother in Bombay.

The Next Aamir Khan?

Meanwhile, *Circus* had put Shah Rukh as a forerunner on the television map. The buzz of his high-voltage performance

---

[11]Shah Rukh repeats his favourite chant in the sports film *Chak De! India,* which went on to become a huge success.

and rapid-fire dialogue delivery was noticed by film-makers in Bombay. His landline in Delhi started ringing incessantly. Producer Harry Baweja was the first to call. Shah Rukh politely rejected the offer, for reasons best known to him.

Around this time, two young Khans, Aamir and Salman, both industry insiders, had become the heartthrobs of the nation. Their virginal, vanilla romances had made them the reigning poster boys. In contrast to their prim and proper image, Shah Rukh was defiantly unkempt, yet ferociously confident about his talent. Unlike these well-manicured heroes, his thick mane of voluminous hair fell uncontrollably on his forehead. So much so that when his friend Vivek Vaswani took Shah Rukh to meet producer G.P. Sippy, the latter exclaimed exasperatedly, 'His hair is like a bloody bear's!' Sippy turned down Vaswani's proposal to make a small-budget film with Aziz Mirza as director and Shah Rukh as hero.

Although the grungy looking Delhi boy from television was not regular hero material, his television buzz superseded that. Raj Kanwar, a new director who had shot with actor Armaan Kohli for the film *Deewana*, approached Shah Rukh to step in for Kohli.

Around the same time, Hema Malini, who had once contacted Shah Rukh in Delhi and said that she liked him for his aristocratic nose, also decided to cast him as the lead in her directorial debut *Dil Aashna Hai*. Director Rajiv Mehra signed him for *Chamatkar* and Rakesh Roshan for *King Uncle*. So widespread was the craze of the *Fauji* boy that Roshan's family had pushed him to cast the unconventional hero.

Soon Shah Rukh's popularity convinced Sippy to change his mind and decide to gamble. He signed Shah Rukh and Aziz Mirza for the film, titled *Raju Ban Gaya Gentleman*.

Vivek Vaswani sweet-talked actress Juhi Chawla, who along with Aamir Khan was a star then, to act opposite the newcomer Shah Rukh. Vaswani told her that Shah Rukh was 'the next Aamir Khan'. Juhi had heard of Shah Rukh, but had not seen *Fauji*. They met on the sets of *Raju Ban Gaya Gentleman*. One look at Shah Rukh's scrawny frame and unruly hair and she turned to Vaswani, exclaiming, 'Eeek! This is the next Aamir Khan!'

First level of mission impossible was complete with five films tucked under his cap. The next was a secret of which only few were aware. Shah Rukh was madly in love with a girl since the time he was eighteen and she was fourteen. Her name was Gauri. He had to now get her from Delhi to Bombay. This was an impossible task, but the 'Deewana' was not going to give up. His heart was set on convincing Gauri, his lady-love, to marry him and come to Bombay.

The nation loved him. But he loved only Gauri.

7

Love Actually

*T*he root of Shah Rukh's love story with Gauri and his swag lay in the coolness quotient of his C Gang.

The C Gang had imbibed its style from the late 1970s film, *Grease*, and had a strong sense of branding. They all wore blue jeans, white T-shirts, Nike shoes and gelled their hair back. Each T-shirt had the C Gang logo and the members' name inscribed on the back. They even inconspicuously wore a small painted C Gang logo on their white school shirt to keep the team spirit going. If it was not for this spirit, and gang buddy Ashok Vassan, Shah Rukh would have never spoken to Gauri.

It all started around 1983, when the eighteen-year-old Shah Rukh had gone to a dance party for the first time in his life. At the party, the boys and girls sat separately. The boys would go up to the girls and ask them for a dance and then they would hit the floor together. Owing to his all-boy schooling, Shah Rukh was too shy to even ask a girl for a dance. He was self-conscious and knew that if she said no to him, he would probably dissipate in embarrassment. So, at the party, he sat quietly but could not stop looking at a girl who sat at the other end of the room. She wasn't conventionally beautiful, but was charming and had a gorgeous figure.

Gauri was fourteen. Though keen to speak to her, Shah Rukh hung on to his reticence and was reluctant to initiate a conversation. That was when Vassan, stepped in to help him.

He asked Gauri if she would dance with Shah Rukh.

Gauri relented and unknowingly became the first girl who spoke to the shy Shah Rukh for more than three seconds. The duo not only enjoyed their dance, but Shah Rukh was completely smitten by her and said to himself, '*Enu kudi leni hai* (This is the girl I would like to make mine).'

Gauri's elegant poise was a perfect match for the zestful Shah Rukh and he was completely love-struck. He asked for her phone number and she was happy to share it with him. He had thought it was going to be a smooth ride here on. But reaching out to her on the landline at home in those days was a task Shah Rukh would have to find a way to overcome.

Gauri lived in a joint family in Panchsheel Park, a posh area in Delhi where the upper class resided in bungalows or row houses, and the British-styled Panchsheel Club was its centre of social buzz. Her parents, Colonel Ramesh Chandra and Savita Chibber, and brother, Vikrant, lived in the same house with her maternal uncle and his family. The large family managed their garment business and the house was always buzzing with family members and domestic helps. A boy calling for her frequently would raise eyebrows in her traditional middle-class family. Thus Shah Rukh requested Gauri's girlfriends to make a call. Soon, the moment Gauri heard 'Shaheen' was calling, she would know that Shah Rukh was waiting to talk to her.

The next stop was for the duo to meet again. The colonial Panchsheel Club was the decided venue. Shah Rukh arrived there on his uncle's tumbledown scooter that he had borrowed for the occasion. Along with him tagged his other C Gang friend, Raman. Shah Rukh and Gauri spent an awkward date sitting at the poolside while Raman temporarily disappeared, allowing the couple a bit of privacy. On the way back, the scooter refused to start. Shah Rukh and Raman had to walk back with the shambled two-wheeler. Shah Rukh was embarrassed and prayed that Gauri had not seen this predicament. He did not want this rundown image to be Gauri's recollection of their first date.

Later, Gauri would meet Shah Rukh at parties. He taught her how to drive and would help with her studies. Some of the naughty things that she would do included jumping over the school walls and running off to meet Shah Rukh.

The first time one of Gauri's friends saw Shah Rukh, he was in red satin shorts, hair covering his eyes and in Shah Rukh's own words, 'resembling a bear'. Her friend had exclaimed, 'Who is this dog that you are looking at?' But soon enough, he had charmed her friends too. He helped choreograph a dance for her friends, who went on to win a competition. Not only that, he helped them with their studies and even taught them economics.

Thorns in the Love Story

The whiff of their relationship had drifted into Gauri's family. The disparity in their living standards, with Shah Rukh having no steady income and living in a miniscule apartment in Rajendra Nagar, was not easy for Gauri's parents to accept. The fact that this was an inter-faith relationship became another thorn in their love story.

Gauri's brother, Vikrant, tried his best to scare Shah Rukh away by telling him stories of their uncle, Tejinder Tiwari, who was a strong man with muscles that 'rippled under moonlight'. But when Vikrant realized that Shah Rukh was unfazed by the threat, he planned to break his legs.

The stage was set. Shah Rukh was to play a hockey match and Vikrant was in the rival team. The buzz had spread that the Chibber boy and his friends were aiming for Shah Rukh's ankles.

During the match, every time Vikrant tried to aim for his legs, Shah Rukh would dodge him and score a goal. This kept happening on a loop and by the end of the match, Shah Rukh scored five goals and managed to get away, unharmed. Later, Shah Rukh humorously mentioned that he let Vikrant off lightly because he was Gauri's brother. But had it been anyone else, he would have easily scored at least twenty goals.

Shah Rukh and Vikrant's friction carried on for a long time. Though Shah Rukh took all of this in his carefree stride, the problems in his own mind were making him restless.

Though on the surface he was a part of the 'cool' C Gang, his middle-class possessiveness started to take a toll on his relationship with Gauri. He objected to her sense of dressing and blithe attitude. Even her leaving her hair untied led to bitter conflict between the two. Swimsuits were a complete taboo and if she so much as spoke to another boy, he would get furious. The list went on and on.

Stifled, Gauri finally decided that she had had enough. For a few months, she avoided Shah Rukh, refusing to meet him or attend the phone when 'Shaheen' called. Then one day, without telling him, she went off for an extended vacation. Her friends too, refused to help any more or tell Shah Rukh where she was. This uncertainty drove him berserk.

But Shah Rukh was not one to be so easily dodged. The obsessive lover called Gauri's house, changed his voice to sound like a girl's, and asked for her. He was quick to find out where she had gone. It was Bombay.

That was the time Shah Rukh revealed his heartbreak to his mother. She gave him some money and asked him to go to Bombay and get his love back. In 1990, Shah Rukh arrived in Bombay with ₹10,000 in his pocket to take Gauri back home.

An upbeat Shah Rukh was accompanied by his friends Benny Thomas and Ashish in this mission. They stayed in a friend's fancy flat in South Bombay. But just when they had begun to settle down, Rahul Mukherjee, the friend who had made this free accommodation available to them, announced that his parents were returning from their vacation.

The boys were out on the streets. Bombay was an expensive city and their funds were fast draining out. Shah Rukh sold his favourite camera to get some more funds. The relentless search carried on as the boys slept on benches and railway platforms, washed in hotel bathrooms, ate food from street stalls, all to search for a girl they only knew had come to this vast city. A girl who their friend could not live without.

The heartbroken Khan and his friends had now started living on cigarettes instead of food. His friend Ashish, particularly, was getting jittery and adamant to return home.

A worn-out Shah Rukh, who had combed the city to find his lady-love, was at his wits' end. He was short of funds, his friends had given up and so he knew he would have to return to Delhi empty-handed. Shah Rukh was angry with how Bombay had treated him. One such day, with an empty pocket, hungry and dejected, he stood at Marine Drive in South Bombay, with the setting sun on his face and declared, 'One day I am going to rule this city.' The gods were listening.

With the last bit of money, they bought train tickets to go back to Delhi but somewhere deep within his heart, Shah Rukh knew he was not going back without his girl.

It was their last day in the bustling city. The only thing he knew for sure was that Gauri loved to swim and so maybe she was near a beach somewhere. They had combed all the South Bombay beaches and now it was time for the North Bombay ones. But Gauri was not there. That's when a local told them that further north, there were a few more beaches. A few hours were left to board the train, his friends were anxious to leave, but Shah Rukh was still looking. Then just like a clichéd film scene, where least expected, Shah Rukh found Gauri at the distant Gorai Beach in the north of Bombay. He thought he had made it and found his love. But Gauri still needed time and space. She wanted a break from their relationship and would let him know if she wished to continue. Shah Rukh returned to Delhi, heartbroken, yet hopeful.

A couple of months later, Gauri sent a message to Shah Rukh. She had made her decision and wanted to meet him. Shah Rukh was apprehensive until she confessed that she had met other boys, but no one was quite like him. They realized that they were meant to be together.

One day, following around two years of dating, Shah Rukh was dropping Gauri at her residence, when he quickly blurted the magical words, 'Will you marry me?' Then just as quickly he drove away, too scared to hear a 'no'.

In a chat show, many years later, Gauri's mother revealed that if she had to choose between Gauri and Shah Rukh to stay with, she would not bat an eyelid before choosing Shah Rukh. But back then, convincing Gauri's family was a nightmare.

Initially, they resorted to juvenile tactics like introducing Shah Rukh to Gauri's family as a Hindu boy, since the religion factor seemed a big obstacle.

Along with the inter-faith issue, Shah Rukh was an aspiring actor. The actor now admits that if a struggling boy came today to ask for his daughter Suhana's hand, he would probably say no too. And that's what Gauri's parents did. But Gauri was adamant and fortunately for her, *Fauji* happened.

Gauri's dad, himself a colonel, was impressed by Shah Rukh's acting skills and his ability to master the portrayal of an army man. One would have thought that now it would be easy for Shah Rukh to walk into their hearts and home. Ironically however, while they loved him as an actor, as a prospective son-in-law, they hated him. Particularly because acting was his choice of profession.

Shah Rukh's career was taking a step forward every day and he was cast as the lead in the television series *Circus*. Being away from Gauri was difficult for him. During the shooting of the series, the actor would coax his co-star Anita Sarin to call Gauri's house and ask for her. As soon as her family handed the phone to Gauri, he would quickly take the receiver from Anita and the love-struck couple would chat away.

Finally, it was Gauri's aunt, Neeru, (the wife of Tejinder, the man whose 'muscles rippled under moonlight') who came to their aid. Gauri and Shah Rukh met Neeru at a restaurant and she interrogated him well. It was almost like a job interview that Shah Rukh passed with flying colours. Neeru edged Tejinder to meet the boy and soon after, Tejinder told his sister and brother-in-law that Shah Rukh was the right match for Gauri.

Once Ramesh and Savita met him, they too fell for his charm.

On 25 October 1991, dressed in a suit, borrowed from the wardrobe of his upcoming film *Raju Ban Gaya Gentleman*, accompanied by his old friends and new ones—Vivek Vaswani and Aziz Mirza—Shah Rukh rode on an elephant to the venue in Delhi, to take his 'dulhania' back home. To Bombay.

It was a day of celebration for Shah Rukh, and yet another significant day in his life that his mother, who had grown enormously fond of Gauri when they had begun dating, never lived to see.

While Shah Rukh was courting Gauri, a young and reticent Aamir Khan was falling in love, again and again.

Wooing the Girl Next Door

The first time he could not even sum up the courage to tell the girl. The second and third times were slightly better but his propositions met with rejections. The fourth attempt was marginally successful. The relationship lasted for a year and the girl eventually told him that she had stopped feeling for him. Devastated, he shaved his hair, just before auditioning for the film *Holi*.

About two years later, Aamir met yet another girl. She was standing at the window of the apartment opposite to Aamir's. The first time their gaze met, Aamir felt something in the air. Soon he started spending more time at the window. Aamir felt this girl, too, was spending a substantial time at visible distance. This, he believed, was a cue for him to talk to her.

But the girl, Reena Dutta, studying statistics at St Xavier's College, had little in common with Aamir. So when Aamir approached her and told her he liked her, her answer was a strict 'no'.

Aamir felt history was going to repeat itself, but he was adamant that he would rewrite it. His sixth sense told him that Reena was attracted to him but was reluctant to admit it. He told her that they could meet again after a couple of days and she could take some time and think about it. Reena was unsure. But Aamir requested her for just two more days. He assured her that if she felt the same after that, he would never pursue her.

Two days later, Reena met Aamir. The writing was on the wall. The answer was 'no'. Aamir, as promised, walked away. He even stopped going to his window. Their love story was done and dusted.

Well, almost.

A couple of months later, Reena met Aamir and told him she wanted to talk to him. It was her turn now to ask the uncomfortable question. Aamir sensed it and tried to make her comfortable. That's when she confessed that she had feelings for Aamir and asked him if he still felt the same for her. An ecstatic Aamir nodded and this laid the foundation for their relationship.

But this love story had its share of problems too. The eternally intense Aamir, to proclaim his love for Reena, wrote a letter in blood to her. He thought it was the perfect way to express his deep love for her. The sensible girl immediately admonished him. He realized that it was not the right thing to do.

Aamir would even sing to her his favourite song, 'Sagar jaisi

Sanjukta Nandy

ankhon wali' from *Saagar*. Reena would like the fact that he sung to her but gently told him that he was an atrocious crooner.

Aamir was not earning and Reena was still a student then. So Reena's parents were disappointed that she was seeing him. The couple was apprehensive that their parents would never approve of their relationship. Thus, a plan was made and they decided to marry secretly.

Runaway Bride and Groom

On 14 March 1986, the day Aamir turned twenty-one, they applied to the marriage registrar's office for a license. A month later, the day the world was busy watching Javed Miandad hit the historical sixer in the last ball against India in Sharjah, the young couple discreetly climbed into Bus Number 21. They crossed the foot bridge at Bandra station and walked into the Griha Nirman Bhavan, to execute their plan.

It took only a box of mithai, some signatures and an exchange of garlands that a few friends had carried. Within fifteen minutes, Aamir and Reena were married and as Aamir later recalled, it cost him only ₹10.

The after-party was held at director Satyajit Bhatkal's house over snacks and cold drinks. A special cake was arranged by Bhatkal's wife, Svati, who was also one of the witnesses at the registration. The couple cut the cake, shared the joy but the party quickly wound up as Bhatkal's mother was supposed to return and all traces of the celebration needed to be wiped clean. The wedding ceremony over, Aamir and Reena went back to their respective houses and continued with their lives.

When Aamir started shooting for *Qayamat Se Qayamat*

Tak, Reena visited the sets in Bombay. They did not breathe a word of their marriage to even their closest family members and everyone thought they were just good friends. During the shooting of the song 'Papa kehte hain', Aamir convinced Mansoor to let Reena lip sync a few lines of the song, as she was present on the set. Reena was initially shy, but Aamir convinced her, saying he wanted to embed their togetherness for eternity. Finally, Reena sang to him, 'Ankhon mein jaadu, honto pe pyar.'

Aamir's little secret was carefully tucked away but despite being the meticulous planner that he was, he could not thwart destiny's counterplan. Due to some local disturbances on the Ooty-Bangalore (now Bengaluru) highway, the unit decided to shift to Bangalore for the outdoor shoot. Back in Bombay, Reena had gone on a college picnic and had promised to call Aamir at his hotel, when she returned home. Since only landlines were existing then, an adamant Aamir refused to leave for the next destination till Reena called. When the unit was restless and refused to delay further, a teary-eyed Aamir finally confided to sister Nuzhat, who helped keep the unit calm. Reena's bus had broken down and it took her more time to reach home than the scheduled plan. Only after Aamir spoke to Reena did he budge and the unit moved on to shoot. But by that time the news of the marriage had percolated to their respective families.

The young daughter-in-law was instantly welcomed into Aamir's family, but the same was not the case with Reena's parents. They needed more time to accept the news. Reena's father, a senior officer in Air India, was so unhappy with the revelation that he fell sick and had to be admitted to a hospital where Aamir quickly visited him. With his courteous approach and honest concern, Aamir won his approval with ease. Years later, one of the happiest moments for Aamir was when Reena's father, tears in his eyes, told him that he could not have chosen a better husband for his daughter. Aamir, too, wept like a baby, when he heard that.

When *Qayamat Se Qayamat Tak* was ready for release, R.R. Pathak, the public relations (PR) officer, who was lining up press interactions and interviews, took Aamir aside and told him to keep the news of his marriage under wraps. The traditional belief was that a married debuting hero would not be able to convince the nation to fall in love with him. Aamir relented since too many careers were at stake and did not want to jeopardize their chances of success.

It did not take the press much time to sniff out this story. A couple of months after the success of the film, the fans woke up to the fact that their romantic icon, who had swept the nation's young feminine hearts, was already taken. Aamir and Reena were both private people and Reena preferred never to speak to the press.

They had an enriching and happy marriage. For the next sixteen years.

The film industry now had a defiant Shah Rukh Khan, who flaunted his love and relationship and an Aamir Khan, who kept his marriage secretly under wraps till the release of his film.

And then there was Salman Khan, who was carefree. He was in no hurry. This Khan was invested in endorsing British singer Cliff Richard's view: 'Son, you are a bachelor boy, and that's the way to stay.'

8

Salman, the Eternal Bachelor Boy?

*D*ecember has always been Salman's month to create an impact.

On a lazy Sunday, 1 December 2013, this Khan set the first television episode of *Koffee with Karan*, Season 4, on fire. It was a poker-faced, humorous declaration from him that did the trick—'I am still a virgin, and I am saving myself for my marriage.' The television rating points (TRPs) shot through the roof.

Later, Salman's brother, Arbaaz Khan's explosive comment that Salman cannot do without sex for a month, grabbed media attention once again.[12] Tabloids could not stop talking about Bollywood's most eligible bachelor boy in his fifties, and his series of romances and heartbreaks.

Cupid had worked well through the pen of the writer's son. Salman had begun writing letters to girls right from his school days. While still at school in Gwalior, Salman had ventured with his friends on a sightseeing trip to Dehradun. The group had gulped down many glasses of jaljeera, a refreshing summer drink, and were desperately looking for a

---

[12]On *Koffee with Karan*'s 100th episode (Season 5, Episode 6, 11 December 2016)

washroom. It was outside the washroom that Salman met a local girl from Dehradun and they started writing letters to each other. Even after he returned from Gwalior, the exchange of letters continued. It went on for almost a year till Salman learnt something that broke his heart and he stopped writing to her. The girl thought of him as a brother.

During his school days, he had a crush on one of his teachers. He used to flirt with her and even dropped her home on his cycle. Incidentally, he had removed the rear carrier of the cycle just to ensure that he got the teacher to sit in front with him. It was just a one-sided infatuation that didn't last for too long either.

'Salman was the leader of the Bandra Boys pack, especially when it came to flaunting his swag with pretty girls,' recalls friend, Shehzad Khan. Those days, they had another friend who owned a Mercedes. The boys had persuaded him and other well-off friends to lend them their flashy cars whenever they wanted to go to a party. Mischievous Salman would happily pass it off as his own car with the girls. To grab further attention, he would not refrain from bragging about being super rich too.

Cupid Strikes

When Salman was all of nineteen, he lost his heart to the beautiful granddaughter of Dadamoni, yesteryear actor, Ashok Kumar. He was often spotted driving a red sports car and waiting at the gates of St Xavier's College, Bombay, where Shaheen Jaffrey, studied.

Shaheen, an ex-model, had some clear Bollywood connections. She was the niece of yesteryear actress, Saira

Banu, while today's young actress Kiara Advani is Shaheen's niece. Kiara validated that her aunt was indeed the first one to steal Salman's heart after she was introduced to Salman by Kiara's mother, who used to be Salman's cycling friend.

It was yet another coincidence that, 'Shaheen' was the code name Shah Rukh and Gauri had coined to avoid family attention and to chat with each other over the telephone during their courtship.

Shaheen and Salman were about to tie the knot when, the Miss India 1980 winner, Sangeeta Bijlani, sashayed into Salman's life. This possibly led to the breakup of the teen romance.

Sangeeta and Salman met at a party in 1988. There was an instant connection and the two were like a house on fire. Sangeeta found Salman to be sensitive, good-looking and a star in the making, while Salman found her to be elegant, sophisticated and extremely attractive. They later went on to work together for a commercial for Lakhani hawai chappals.

Their relationship continued for almost six years during which the fashionista, Sangeeta, was one of the pivotal reasons for Salman's transformation into a style icon. The two were inseparable as they socialized and holidayed together, their favourite destination being Goa. Sangeeta blended in with Salman's family and became one of them.

In a 1993 interview, Salman had said, 'Yes, I plan to marry. When the time comes, I will. It could be to Sangeeta (Bijlani) or to anybody else.'[13] And exactly a year later, the two decided

---

[13]*India Today* Web Desk, 'Throwback: When Salman Khan wanted to marry Sangeeta Bijlani', *India Today*, 24 May 2018, accessed 9 September 2019, https://www.indiatoday.in/movies/gossip/story/throwback-thursday-when-salman-khan-wanted-to-marry-sangeeta-bijlani-1240335-2018-05-24

Sanjukta Nandy

to get married. The wedding date was set for 27 May 1994.

Preparations were in full swing. But about a month before D-Day, Sangeeta had begun to feel that something was not right. What she found out made her realize that this relationship was not meant to culminate into marriage. A Pakistani model, Somy Ali, had stirred Salman's heart and he was cheating on Sangeeta with her.[14]

Sangeeta had taken Shaheen's place in Salman's heart and now Somy Ali had taken Sangeeta's. Though the invites were printed, the wedding was called off at the last moment. It is common knowledge that Sangeeta was not ready to accept Salman's infidelity. This remained the closest the bachelor boy ever came to tying the knot.

Reportedly, it was not only infidelity but also bouts of aggression from Salman that propelled Sangeeta to take this tough call. Once, in a fit of fury he had broken her leg. Sangeeta described her relationship with Salman Khan as her 'most emotionally traumatic experience ever'[15]. Years later, though, she became good friends with Salman and his family.

Salman and Somy were inseparable for the next few years. As intense as their love was the obsessive possessiveness. Brutally expressive about his dislikes, once Salman reportedly did not approve of Somy enjoying a drink at a party. To show his displeasure, he picked up the glass and poured the entire drink on her head. Somy was shocked and humiliated, yet it was not this, but the entry of a green-eyed Miss World, into Salman's life that drove their relationship to the rocks.

---

[14]Ibid.

[15]*Itimes*, 'Salman Khan crimes that were never reported', Indiatimes.com, 25 July 2016, accessed September 2019, https://www.indiatimes.com/culture/who-we-are/salman-khan-crimes-that-were-never-reported-277603.html#2

KHANtastic

A story published during that time in *Stardust* magazine, declared that Somy had no idea what was brewing between Salman and Aishwarya Rai (now Aishwarya Rai Bachchan). Salman was already a superstar by then and speculations about his wedding to girlfriend Somy Ali were doing the rounds. Once Somy got to know about his new link-up, she broke up with him and left India to settle down in the United States. Somy had taken Sangeeta's place in Salman's heart and now Aishwarya took Somy's.

Miss India to Miss World

Salman and Aishwarya's romance bloomed on the sets of Sanjay Leela Bhansali's *Hum Dil De Chuke Sanam*. Like his previous girlfriends, Aishwarya too became a regular visitor at Salman's house and got very close to his family. She had won the Miss World title in 1994, had made her film debut with Mani Ratnam's *Iruvar* in 1997, but till she met Salman, she had no box-office hits to her credit. The whiff in the press was that a smitten Salman had recommended her to Bhansali and to other directors. *Hum Dil De Chuke Sanam* catapulted Aishwarya to new heights of fame and sealed her position as the queen of Salman's heart.

Aishwarya became a part of Salman's family and their celebrations. His sisters, Alvira and Arpita, became her buddies and her relationship with Salman dug a strong foundation. But news was rife that Aishwarya's parents were not happy with this relationship and yet she rebelled against them. She moved into a separate apartment in Gorakh Hill Tower, Lokhandwala.

But in March 2002, it was all over. Aishwarya declared in an *Indian Express* interview, 'I stood by him, enduring his alcoholic misbehaviour in its worst phases and in turn, I was at the receiving end of his abuse (verbal, physical and emotional), infidelity and indignity. That is why, like any other self-respecting woman, I ended my relationship with him.'[16]

What led this fairy-tale romance to take a turn to doomsday by 2002? Salman's family, specially his brother, Sohail, supported his brother and came out to say that Salman was insecure that Aishwarya would not acknowledge their relationship, even though she was well embedded into his life. So perhaps, insecurity led to volatility, and like his previous relationships, marked the beginning of Salman's obsessive, aggressive wrath in his relationship with Aishwarya.

One incident that deepened the crack in the relationship was when on a November night in 2001, Salman, in a fit of fury, reached Aishwarya's Gorakh Hill Tower apartment. What he did there made tabloid headlines.

It was reported that a possibly inebriated Salman arrived at Aishwarya's apartment, which was on the seventeenth floor, late in the night. She would not open the door, so he kept banging on it. When she did not open after hours of his banging, he is alleged to have threatened to jump off the building. Salman was seething with anger and this carried on up until almost 3 a.m. Aishwarya did finally relent and allowed him in. Sources close to Salman however opined that Salman wanted a promise of marriage, but Aishwarya, who was then stepping up the success ladder, was not keen to commit.

During this incident, the scared neighbours did not call

---

[16]Team MyNation, 'Shocking throwback: 10 reasons why Aishwarya Rai broke up with Salman Khan', My Nation, 26 March 2019, accessed 9 September 2019, https://www.mynation.com/entertainment/shocking-throwback-10-reasons-why-aishwarya-rai-broke-up-with-salman-khan-poymqr

KHANtastic

the cops but it is believed that Aishwarya's father complained to the police about this incident. This drama publicly declared the rift between Salman and Aishwarya, which till then was marked as alleged rumours. Since this event, their relationship rapidly went downhill. This crack further deepened when Salman's ex-girlfriend Somy Ali called him to request help for her father's surgery. Salman not only agreed to help her but without informing Aishwarya, flew to the United States to be by Somy's side.

Aishwarya was livid, but Salman managed to make truce. But with trust broken and doubt ripping their relationship apart, the truce soon went out of the window. News surfaced that Salman had created a ruckus on the set of her movie *Kuch Naa Kaho*. Abhishek Bachchan, whom Aishwarya married much later, was acting opposite her in the film. Salman, reportedly, not only created havoc during the shooting but even damaged Aishwarya's car.[17]

The list of Salman's unpredictable behaviour began to snowball and reached its peak on the sets of his now friend Shah Rukh's home production *Chalte Chalte*, where Aishwarya was cast in the lead.

A unit member of *Chalte Chalte* revealed that the unit after completing the filming of a song sequence from Malshet, headed out at night for the next location, near Pune. That is when Salman appeared on the shoot and created a scene. For nearly four and a half hours, he was uncontrollable and

[17]DNA Web Team, 'When Aishwarya Rai Bachchan confessed, "The chapter of Salman Khan was a nightmare in my life"', DNA India, 7 April 2019, accessed September 2019, https://www.dnaindia.com/bollywood/photo-gallery-when-aishwarya-rai-bachchan-confessed-the-chapter-of-salman-khan-was-a-nightmare-in-my-life-2737317

tried to drag Aishwarya away. This ticked director Aziz Mirza off and he called off the shoot as well as the schedule. The next day, Aishwarya called producer Shah Rukh to apologize for the fiasco and so did Salman. But director Mirza was apprehensive to shoot with the love interest of an impulsive man and Shah Rukh was in two minds. Aishwarya lost the role and it eventually went to Rani Mukerji.

After Aishwarya confirmed her break-up with Salman in 2002, she said that he wasn't able to come to terms with it. However, she was sure of her decision as she stated that the Salman chapter was the worst in her life, and that she was glad she was out of it.

Even after the break-up, Salman would call her and have unpleasant spats. He would suspect her of having affairs with her co-stars. He even kicked up a storm with her co-star Vivek Oberoi, who she was said to be dating after Salman. Aishwarya and Vivek met on the sets of *Kyun! Ho Gaya Na...* in 2004 and reportedly grew closer. Vivek claimed that one night Salman telephoned him forty-one times and threatened to kill him. Salman, of course, denied these allegations. The actress, who was then undergoing treatment for a hairline fracture of her ankle at Mumbai's Hinduja Hospital, got totally fed up and issued her own statement[18]: 'I have categorically declined to work with Mr Salman Khan...and my family is witness... For the sake of my well-being, my sanity, my dignity and the dignity and self-respect of my family—ENOUGH! I will not work with Mr Salman Khan. The Salman chapter was a nightmare in my life and I am thankful to God that it is over!'

[18]Rediff, 'Enough!' 7 April 2003, accessed September 2019, https://www.rediff.com/movies/2003/apr/07ash.htm

Salman never admitted to have physically attacked Aishwarya. He told *Mid-Day* in an interview on 18 September 2002, 'No. I have never beaten her. Anyone can beat me up. Any fighter here on the sets can thrash me. That is why people are not scared of me. I do get emotional. Then I hurt myself. I have banged my head against the wall. I have hurt myself all over. I cannot hurt anyone else.'

After their break-up, Salman in his next film, *Lucky: No Time for Love*, in 2005, cast the Aishwarya doppelgänger, Sneha Ullal. This caught the media's attention but did not qualify for the label of a love story. Though media did try to dig out some smoke, not much was discovered.

Quintessentially Bollywood

The next to deeply stir Salman's heart was British model Katrina Turquotte, now popularly known as Katrina Kaif. Salman later spoke about his thoughts when he first met Katrina, 'It was a small get-together. She had come home for a party and I thought she was one of the sweetest girls ever. She knew my sisters and all my friends. But she didn't know me.' Although the two never came out in the open about their relationship, Katrina's closeness with Salman was never hidden. They were often seen taking a bike ride together in Bandstand and Katrina was also very close to the Khan's family. The two churned electrifying chemistry on screen too.

Off screen, their favourite hangout was the Barista coffee shop at Bandstand where Salman had instructed the owner and staff that they should not leak the duo's whereabouts to anyone, especially the media. Eyewitnesses reveal, that one day while they were chatting, Salman grew aggressive and then there was a sound of a crackling slap. Salman had landed one on Katrina's cheek, due to his possessiveness, this time regarding Katrina's passionate scenes with actor Akshay Kumar in their latest film.[19]

Back in 2007, when Katrina made an appearance on Karan Johar's show, *Koffee with Karan,* Johar asked what her response would be if Salman ever asked her to marry him. She had lost her train of thoughts for a moment and sat still. She did not reply.

After a considerably choppy relationship which fuelled rumour mills long enough, Katrina was seen with the much younger, Ranbir Kapoor. Salman is reported to have had abusive episodes with Ranbir too. He once again cast a Katrina doppelgänger, Zarine Khan, in films opposite him. However, even when Katrina had an Income Tax raid in January 2011, Salman defended her on Twitter, taking her side.[20]

It is Bollywood folklore that ironically when Katrina wanted to break up with Ranbir, she went to Salman for advice. Katrina and Salman became friends again. They were yet again busy setting the silver screen on fire. Sangeeta and Somy, too, remained friends with Salman and his family.

Today, Salman is often seen at private and public gatherings with the Romanian beauty, Lulia Vântur, who says that Salman Khan is a 'very special person' in her life. She is often spotted with Salman at film shoots, parties and family occasions. The tabloids are waiting to get their keyboards clicking with another

---

[19]Itimes, 'Salman Khan crimes that were never reported', Indiatimes, 25 July 2016, accessed 3 March 2019, https://www.indiatimes.com/culture/who-we-are/salman-khan-crimes-that-were-never-reported-277603.html#9

[20]*India Today,* 'Salman Khan voices concern for his ex Katrina Kaif on twitter', 29 January 2011, accessed September 2019, https://www.indiatoday.in/movies/celebrities/story/salman-khan-voices-concern-for-his-ex-katrina-kaif-on-twitter-127539-2011-01-29

KHANtastic

love story and the nation's most often asked question remains: When will Salman Khan marry?

Salim Khan, his father, sums up his own thesis on Salman's bachelorhood. He is convinced that initially Salman falls for the girls he works with. They are ambitious, beautiful, career-driven individuals. But then he looks for his mother in them. And that's where the trouble starts. The bachelor boy seconds his father on this and laments, 'They don't make any more like her. *Bhagwan ne dye tod di* (God has destroyed the dye after creating my mother).'

Salman had confessed once that there was a time he wanted to get married. He had come close to tying the knot a couple of times, but then more than often, the other half would get cold feet. On a lighter note, he had said, 'They feel boyfriend *theek hai, par isko zindagi bhar jhelna padega kya?* (It is fine to have him as a boyfriend but how am I going to deal with him all my life?)'

Like Bollywood love stories, Salman's relationships had all the elements of romance, obsession, regrets and heartbreaks. Somewhere he believed that when in love, a couple naturally fights and that's probably been his poison. He has had many a fairy-tale romance but nothing lasted for ever. Two noted beauty pageant winners and a couple of more stunning actresses, all of who happened to be Salman's various love interests, at different times of his life, had something similar to say. He was one of the best as well as one of the worst things to happen to them.

Hence, was it a toss between impulse or anger, or a generous dose of both, that gave Salman the iconic bachelor-boy status, making him Bollywood's most eligible bachelor and controversy's favourite child?

Sanjukta Nandy

9

The Angry Pathans

*T*he street near Galaxy Apartments, Salman's home, was quiet and peaceful that night till a police van headed towards the house. Unaware, Salman was sleeping in his ground-floor apartment, when his mother, Salma, woke him up with bad news. She had seen the police vehicle approaching their building and panicked.

She nudged him hastily and asked in a tone of fear, 'What have you done now?'

Salman drowsily mumbled, 'I have not done anything I know. I am sleeping now.'

But the information sunk into his mind. He woke up with a start and called his staff, Mohan and Dilip, and asked them, '*Aisa kuch hua hai kya*? (Has anything wrong happened?)'

They confirmed that all was good.

Still at the edge of her nerves, Salma prodded, 'Then why has the police come to the building?'

Salman gathered himself and mumbled, 'But what can I do if the police has come to the building?'

His heart still beating a tad faster than usual.

The police had actually come to another apartment in the same building to attend to a fire complaint. Such was the toxic paranoia of Salman getting into trouble with the police and the innumerable criminal charges, that his mother had taken for granted that police in their building meant that Salman was the source of the trouble.

It was not only the fragile heart of a mother that rocked in fear of what trouble Salman would be in now, but even that of his father, who is considered to be the He-Man of the family, that was wilting. Salim Khan is the go-to person in the large Khan family. Whenever the family faces a crisis, everyone looks up to him and he is quick to reassure them with a strong belief, '*Kuch nahi, sab theek ho jayega* (Everything will be fine)'. But Salim Khan recalls that there was a day when he too went weak emotionally because of Salman.

Salman was in Jodhpur Jail in August 2007 for the blackbuck poaching case of 1998 and Salim saab had gone to meet his son along with Salma. As the parents waited for the son to come into the meeting area, Salim saab advised his wife not to bare her emotions in front of Salman. As they were talking, they heard the cops shout out, '343 *ko leke aao* (Get 343 here)'.

When the police opened the door and ushered in 343, the parents saw Salman standing there. He had an unshaved look, with ruffled hair and tired eyes.

Salim saab again whispered to his wife, 'Do not to break down.' But the mother could not hold back her tears. She took off her glasses and started wiping her moist eyes. Salman was allowed to meet them for a brief time and then taken away.

Salim saab returned to the hotel and sat down to have his drink. Like a flash, right in front of his eyes, the heart-wrenching scene at the jail began playing out. Within moments, the father realized that his cheeks were moist. His expression of stoic silence remained unchanged but involuntary tears kept rolling down his face. The Iron Man of the Khan family had crumbled seeing his son in such deep misery.

A superstar in the making: Director Yash Chopra and Shah Rukh on the sets of Darr

On the sets of Baazi: *Aamir faces the camera with co-star Mamta Kulkarni*

Aamir sharing a candid Page 3 moment with his Bollywood leading ladies Preity Zinta, Katrina Kaif and Anushka Sharma, and director Karan Johar

Together we stand: Shah Rukh and Aamir in a joint press conference

Jab We Met: Young Kareena Kapoor on the sets of Andaz Apna Apna, *where she had come to meet Salman, her sister Karisma's co-star then*

On the sets of Andaz Apna Apna: *the Khans set their focus on making a cult comedy*

Aamir celebrating the success of Rangeela *with superstar Amitabh Bachchan, Jaya Bachchan and Aamir's then wife, Reena Dutta*

Mentor and his prodigy: Salman with a young Hrithik Roshan getting ready to face a tsunami of ups and downs that was to follow

Power couples of Mumbai: Mukesh Ambani, Aamir, Kiran Rao and Nita Ambani

The baton of stardom passes on to the Khans: Salman and Aamir with the iconic Dilip Kumar

We are family: (left to right) Aayush Sharma (Salman's sister Arpita's husband), Sohail, Salman, Helen, Salim Khan and Salma Khan

Partners in spinning hits: Director David Dhawan and Salman

Salman and Shah Rukh on the sets of Karan Arjun *with director Rakesh Roshan*

Final touches: Salman with his make-up man Raju Nag, who has been his loyalist for over three decades

Shah Rukh and Salman on a sports drive

A Kodak moment: Shah Rukh and Gauri share a light moment with Aamir at a Bollywood bash

The Hunter becomes the Hunted

Big trouble had begun in 1998, when an FIR was registered in the Kankani Poaching case on 2 October that year. Poonam Chand and Chogaram, from the Bishnoi sect, who were witnesses to the crime had registered a report against Salman and his co-stars of *Hum Saath-Saath Hain*. Salman was arrested in Jodhpur on 12 October 1998, for poaching two blackbucks.

Tabloids reported that trouble had started brewing days ago when Salman had arrived at Jodhpur's Umaid Bhawan Hotel, in an extremely foul mood. He was haughty with the hotel staff, often strutted bare-bodied along the hotel corridors and played cowboy with his co-star, Saif Ali Khan. Pumped with laddish machismo, they lined up soft drink bottles, drew their guns and did target practice. Unfortunately, it did not remain restricted to that.

According to information gathered by *India Today*, the hunting game had begun on the evening of 26 September 1998.[21] Dushyant Singh, a local who then looked after Travelaide, a tour company owned by Gaj Singh, the erstwhile ruler of Jodhpur, had instructed driver Dulani to arrange for sightseeing for some of the guests. Dulani was happily surprised that one of his guests was none other than superstar, Salman Khan. Salman asked if he could drive the Gypsy and Dulani complied. Salman drove, with co-star Satish Shah sitting in front, while Dulani and four others sat behind. One of them, Yashpal, guided Salman towards Bavad village, off Nagaur road, 40 km away

---

[21]Prashant Pandya, 'A Real Story Behind the Black Buck Case of Salman Khan?' 6 April 2018, accessed 19 September 2019, https://myindiamake. com/2018/04/06/a-real-story-behind-the-black-buck-case-of-salman-khan

KHANtastic

from Umaid Palace. A herd of chinkaras were grazing there, unaware of what was to follow.

Dulani's statement later said that Salman fired twice at the animals but missed the target. Satish Shah egged him on, saying, '*Jama ke lagao* (Do it properly).' The third shot proved fatal. Salman got down from the vehicle and slit the chinkara's throat and then, after killing another one, drove back to the hotel. Yashpal then took the car to another hotel, managed to get the kitchen opened at 2.30 in the morning and asked Dulani to leave. The chinkaras were cooked late at night.

Next day, on 27 September, Dulani cleaned the vehicle of dust and blood, the hunt resumed but no deer was found. The following day, Salman, driving with Saif and Dushyant, seemed to be satisfied chasing chinkaras till they tired out, could run no longer, and then shot them.

But what happened on 1 October is what got the actors into deep trouble. This time they got caught. As per the reconstruction of the episode by Rajasthan district and sessions judge, D.N. Joshi, it was brought to light that the stars, who had arrived for shooting of the Rajshri Productions' feel-good film, *Hum Saath-Saath Hain,* had ventured out to hunt fourteen times till 1 October, but no one was caught. That night, Salman, Saif, and actresses Tabu, Neelam and Sonali Bendre set off, in a white gypsy (number: RJ 191C 2201), accompanied by a certain Harish, who had driven them on some of their earlier forays as well.[22]

When they reached a particular stretch of forest—5 km

---

[22]Archana Jahagirdar, 'Buck Stops Shooting Star', *Outlook*, 26 October 1998, accessed 19 September 2019, https://www.outlookindia.com/magazine/story/buck-stops-shooting-stars/206428

Sanjukta Nandy

off the Jodhpur-Mumbai highway and 30 kms from Jodhpur—they spotted a herd of the endangered blackbucks. Salman, who was driving with Saif beside him, stopped, took aim and managed to shoot one blackbuck on the leg. As soon as the first shot was fired, trouble began. Animal-loving Bishnois, who lived close by, rushed out of their houses. The stars fled the scene but stopped a short distance from there. They spotted another herd. Egged on by the actresses seated at the back, Salman was handed the gun and he took another shot, injuring a blackbuck on the neck.

The Bishnois gave them a chase—seven of them on three motorcycles. Salman rushed towards Lunii, a nearby village where the unit had been filming, then changed his mind, turned around and sped towards the safety of Jodhpur instead.

Sixty-eight-year-old Bhenpa Ram, who chased Salman stated, 'I was sleeping when I heard the gunshot. I had a stick with me and I chased them for six and a half kilometres. They saw me chasing and banged my motorcycle. I fell down but I noted down the Gypsy number.'

The Bishnois first filed a complaint with the flying squad of the forest department. 'But when the authorities didn't react for three days, we took to the streets,' said Ram Singh Bishnoi, pradhan of the Akhil Bhartiya Bishnoi Mahasabha.

This was the turning point of royal trouble for the Khan and his co-stars. Killing the blackbuck and chinkara, both Schedule 1 animals on the endangered list, is a violation of the Wildlife Protection Act 1972, and promises the accused anywhere from one to seven years in prison and a fine of not less than ₹10,000.[23]

---

[23] Sobita Dhar, 'Blood Sport', *Outlook*, 27 June 2005, accessed 19 September

KHANtastic

On 12 October, Salman was arrested and charged. The actor just sat there with his face buried in his hands as arguments over his remand continued. The three actresses wept on interrogation, revealing that they had accompanied Salman but tearfully stated, 'We did go there but never shot. We only clapped.' This answer got them off. Saif was let off too. All of them left for Mumbai, leaving Salman at the brunt of the drama and with a bill of ₹15.50 lakh for the producers to pay up.[24]

Although first time on searching the rooms of the actors in Umaid Bhawan, nothing was found, in the second search two air guns (one from Salman's and another from Saif's room) and a camera with a film, which reportedly had pictures of them on the hunt, were recovered. A pistol was also recovered from Mumbai.

In an interview with *The Times of India* in 2012, an angry Salman said, '*Kisi ke baare mein koi bhi bolega...except jo phansa hua hai, woh apne defence mein nahi bol sakta, ki aisa nahi, aisa hua thaa...arre main to tha bhi nahi wahan par*! (Anyone has the right to speak about any person, except the one who is accused. He cannot say anything in his defence. The truth is I was not even present there!)[25]

2019, https://www.outlookindia.com/magazine/story/blood-sport/227749

[24]Rohit Parihar, 'From the archives: Salman gets caught in a widening whirlpool of votes and politics', Indiatoday.in, 26 October 1998, accessed September 2019, https://www.indiatoday.in/magazine/crime/story/19981026-blackbuck-case-salman-khan-caught-in-a-widening-whirlpool-of-votes-politics-827257-1998-10-26

[25]Ananya Bhatacharya, 'Black Buck Poaching case: What Salman Khan says happened that day', *India Today*, 5 April 2018, accessed 9 September 2019, https://www.indiatoday.in/movies/celebrities/story/blackbuck-poaching-case-what-salman-khan-says-happened-that-day-1205306-2018-04-05

Sanjukta Nandy

After twenty years of a gruelling battle through police stations, jails and courts, on 5 April 2018, finally, Salman was fined ₹10,000 and sentenced to five years of jail.

But only for forty-eight hours. On 7 April 2018, he was granted bail by a district and sessions court in Jodhpur. The case still goes on.

Woes of the Volatile Khan

The sparks of Salman's violent image were witnessed by few even during his struggling days. He was known for his dichotomy of personality, large-heartedness interspersed with mercurial, temperamental fluctuations. This got him banned by the press on different occasions.

Well-known journalist Ali Peter John has reported a few eyewitness events that highlight the angry-man impulse of Salman. During the shooting of Salman's first film *Biwi Ho To Aisi*, a curious John had visited the set on director J.K. Bihari's invitation. The director was proud of having given a break to a young boy called Salman Khan, the eldest son of celebrity writer, Salim Khan. John recalls,

> I was interested. I wanted to see how the son of the handsome Salim Khan looked like. I was invited by Bihari to watch the shooting of his film while this new boy, Salman, was shooting with Rekha. Bihari introduced me to the young Khan. He was lean, short, not so good looking and had very long hair, like it was the trend and style among boys of his age. The young and brash Khan just shook my hand. I later came to know that he told Bihari not to invite these '*faltoo*' (useless) press

people during the time he was shooting because they only specialized in writing nonsense and Salman didn't like these people as his father has advised him to keep away from them.

This alienated the journalist and he decided to keep away from the budding Khan for a while.

The journalist's second encounter with Salman landed the Khan into severe trouble, this time with the entire media fraternity. Salman was, by then, the heartthrob and the poster boy of the nation after the runaway hit, *Maine Pyar Kiya*. This incident took place at Filmalaya Studio, during the shoot of the film *Suryavanshi* in 1992. Noted director Rakesh Kumar, known for his hits with Amitabh Bachchan such as *Mr. Natwarlal*, *Yaarana* and *Khoon Pasina*, had invited the journalist who went there with his photojournalist friend, R.D. Rai. A typical fight sequence was being picturized with the action director in charge. The young Khan's handsome face was smudged with tomato ketchup, as blood, and Mr Rai got into action. He meticulously started shooting every moment that his camera could capture. Noticing this, Salman angrily asked him not to take pictures of his 'blood-splattered' face. But the photographer told him, '*Aap apna kaam karo, main mera kaam karke jaaunga* (You do your work, I will do mine and leave).'

This sentence infuriated Salman and he rushed towards the photographer with his fists clenched and abused him in the most foul manner. He then snatched the camera from Rai's hands, pulled out the reel he had shot and asked the photographer to leave the set. Salman told the producer, he would not shoot as long as the photographer was around. Even after being told that both the journalist and the photographer were there by invitation, Salman kept muttering insulting words. Kumar tried to make peace between them. It was not to be and the journalists left. But no one expected what would follow.

The journalist, the photographer and the media did not take this insult lightly. Salman was banned from newspapers and it was decided that no photographs, not even stills from films, and no articles about the rising Khan would be published until he tendered an apology. The rest of the press supported this decision too. The press decided to stay away from all the functions where Salman was expected. Some of them even went to the extent of asking producers to get him out of a frame if they wanted their picture to be published.[26]

This ban continued for years till the Rajshris, who were making *Hum Aapke Hain Koun..!* appealed to the press to support them and the film. It was the goodwill of the Rajshris that ended this ban and bailed Salman back into the tabloids.

Years later, another ban from the press was triggered. During the promotions of *Kick* in 2014, Salman was banned by lensmen because of his attitude towards the press during the promotion of the film. According to reports, the paparazzi decided to boycott Salman after they were reportedly mistreated by his team at a promotional event for the film. To add fuel to fire, the actor laughed about this on his Twitter handle and it did not go down well with the press. But a news-hungry media and a hot-blooded superstar cannot be separated for long. Truce was soon made.

---

[26]BollywoodHungama, 'Throwback Thursday: When Salman Khan was banned by the Press', *The Free Press Journal*, 29 November 2018, accessed 19 September 2019, https://www.freepressjournal.in/entertainment/throwback-thursday-when-salman-khan-was-banned-by-the-press

KHANtastic

In April 2019, journalist Ashok Shyamlal Pandey filed a police complaint against Salman for misbehaviour. He reported that even though he had taken Salman's permission to film him, he and his bodyguards got angry with Pandey and they snatched his phone. However, an onlooker supported Salman and revealed that even after politely telling Pandey not to shoot Salman cycling, the stubborn paparazzi affiliate continued with his endeavours. That's when Salman took away his phone but later asked his bodyguard to return it to the man.[27]

The tug of war between the Khan and the press continues and so does the woes of the volatile Khan. But the most controversial event of Salman's life, that once again shot him into the headlines for the wrong reasons, took place in September 2002.

Reportedly, on 27 September 2002, at about 9.30 p.m., Salman, his friend, singer Kamaal Khan,[28] and an unarmed bodyguard, police constable Ravindra Patil, headed out to Rain Bar in Juhu. From there, the Khans went to JW Marriot, a short distance away. The friends left from the hotel in the wee hours of 28 September to head back home. A few minutes later, Salman's Toyota Land Cruiser had rammed into a bakery in Bandra, injuring four and killing one labourer, all sleeping on the pavement.[29]

Salman later stated that since his driver Altaf was unwell

[27]*Outlook* Web Bureau, 'Journalist accuses Salman of Snatching Phone, Files Police Complaint', *Outlook*, 26 April 2019, accessed 19 September 2019, https://www.outlookindia.com/website/story/india-news-journalist-accuses-salman-khan-of-snatching-phone-files-police-complaint/329322

[28]Kamaal Khan sang the famous Salman-number, 'O o jaane jana'

[29]PTI, '2002 hit-and-run case', *India Today*, 26 December 2012, accessed 19 September 2019, https://www.indiatoday.in/movies/celebrities/story/salman-khan-may-appear-in-court-2002-hit-and-run-case-125388-2012-12-26

Sanjukta Nandy

and had left for the day, he had waited at the driver's seat with the air-conditioner switched on for the other driver, Ashok Singh, to arrive and take them home. But after the crash, eye witness Ravindra Patil's statement said that it was a drunk Salman at the wheels and he was driving at a rash speed of 90 to 100 km per hour. Salman's statement differed, saying that it was Ashok Singh at the wheel and that he was driving safe at a speed of 30 km per hour. The tyre had suddenly burst and this led to the fatal crash.

After the accident, a frenzied crowd, armed with rods and stones, reached the spot. Salman and Kamaal left the spot but only after instructing his driver, Ashok, to call the cops. Patil however claimed differently in his statement. According to him, it was he who had informed the police-control room and they arrived within five minutes.

What ensued after that was another gruelling legal battle for almost thirteen years till the Bombay High Court finally passed the verdict on Bollywood's most controversial Khan. In December 2015, Justice A.R. Joshi, concluded and pronounced the judgement that the prosecution had not established its case against the actor beyond a reasonable doubt, as is required under criminal law.[30] Salman was acquitted from all criminal charges that he had been held guilty of by a trial court in May 2015, with respect to the crash. He was also absolved from the charges of leaving the accident spot without providing aid to the victims.

After the acquittal, Bollywood's enfant terrible wept

---

[30]Swati Deshpande, 'Salman Khan Acquitted of All Charges in Hit and Run Case', *The Times of India*, 10 December 2015, accessed 9 September 2019, https://timesofindia.indiatimes.com/india/Salman-Khan-acquitted-of-all-charges-in-hit-and-run-case/articleshow/50120366.cms

KHANtastic

uncontrollably for several minutes. Minutes later, he was heard humming a tune of relief.

While Salman's escapades were becoming folklore, in Bandstand, a walking distance from Salman's Galaxy Apartments, now lived another Khan, this one known for his courteous demeanour and humble attitude.

But underneath this personality, by his own admission, he was a hot-blooded Pathan and he was soon finding himself at the epicentre of controversies, his reckless image walking hand in hand with incidents of volatility.

Travails of Another Hot-blooded Pathan

Coincidentally enough, the media that eats out of the palm of his hand today, is the one with whom Shah Rukh had his first brash encounter in Mumbai. In 1992, he was to shoot an explicit scene with his leading lady Deepa Sahi, for Ketan Mehta's film, *Maya Memsaab*. It was reported and published by a leading magazine, *Cine Blitz*,[31] that it was director Mehta's idea that Deepa and Shah Rukh should spend the night at a suburban hotel. This would help them shed their inhibition for the shoot. It was reported that the lead actors complied to it. Shah Rukh, who used to shy away from even clicking pictures off screen with his heroines then, was livid at this

---

[31]Puri, 'SRK Was ARRESTED! When A FAKE Story On Shahrukh Khan Spending A Night With An Actress Was Published', Filmibeat, 3 November 2017, accessed 12 June 2019, https://www.filmibeat.com/bollywood/features/2017/when-a-fake-story-on-shahrukh-khan-spending-a-night-with-deepa-sahi-was-published-srk-arrested-269242.html

publish. The name of the article's author was not mentioned in the magazine.

Soon enough, sizzling with latent anger, Shah Rukh met Keith D'Costa, a *Cine Blitz* journalist, at a function and impulsively assumed that he was the author of the insulting allegation. Just like Thor's sledgehammer, Mjölnir, falls on the black hats, the choicest of abuses rained from the actor, scorching the scene. Shah Rukh followed this up by calling D'Costa's landline number and threatened to go to his house and beat him up. Not stopping at that, he actually landed up at the journalist's house where he verbally abused him and even threatened to castrate him in front of his parents.

On counsel of his editor, D'Costa filed a complaint at the Bandra Police Station and Shah Rukh was summoned to the station. Luckily, courtesy his star status, he was not shoved into the lockup. As a matter of fact, some cops, overjoyed at seeing him, even took his autograph. Shah Rukh then requested to make a phone call and was allowed to do so. The call was made, not to his lawyer or his friends, but to his sworn enemy, D'Costa.

Right in front of the policemen, he once again threatened D'Costa, saying, 'I am in jail now, but I will come out and f**k you.' Late that night, Shah Rukh's friend, Chikki Panday, got him out on bail.

However, two years later, when another *Cine Blitz* journalist, Virginia Vacha, assured Shah Rukh that D'Costa was not the author of this article, he not only met D'Costa and hugged him but was also ready to apologize to his parents for having threatened their son in front of them. All was well with the magazine and the star henceforth.

Much later in life, in 2012, King Khan did have another

episode of volatile outburst, surprisingly with the husband of one of his closest friends in the industry, Farah Khan, a friend whose kanyadaan (giving away the bride) was done by none other than Shah Rukh himself.

This was a short while after Shah Rukh's mega, superhero film, *Ra.One* had not fared well at the theatres and the superstar was not at his cheerful best. Film director Farah Khan's editor-director husband, Shirish Kunder, who is known for his razor-sharp opinions on social media, tweeted in October 2011: 'I just heard a 150-crore firework fizzle.' It did not take much time for the industry to realize that it was hinted at the mega-budget Diwali release which had damp collections at the box office. Shah Rukh did not publicly retaliate but the ripple effect did show up at Sanjay Dutt's success party of *Agneepath* held at Juhu's then popular nightclub, Aurus, in January 2012.

It was reported that Shah Rukh came to the nightclub in the wee hours of Monday morning. He was in a good mood. He hit the dance floor with Sanjay and his wife, Manyata, and the celebrations continued with the clicking of pictures.

An eyewitness at the party later revealed that Shirish hovered around Shah Rukh and followed him onto the dance floor. Initially, the actor ignored him, but things took a turn for the worse when Sanjay Dutt escorted Shah Rukh out of the venue to introduce him to a close friend. Kunder went right behind Shah Rukh and murmured something in his ear. This finally broke the boundary of Shah Rukh's patience. He turned around and holding Kunder by the scruff of his neck, forced him to sit on the sofa near the nightclub's exit. Heated words were followed by a slap that echoed into the headlines the next day.[32]

---

[32]TNN, 'Why Shah Rukh Khan slapped Farah Khan's husband Shirish

The following day, Farah sent out a bulk SMS to the media that stated, 'Shah Rukh has always told me that physical abuse is the worst way to sort out a problem. It saddens me to see him doing the same.'

Celebrity photographer Dabboo Ratnani tweeted: 'I was present at Sanju's party and without any bias fully support Shah Rukh.' Later, in August 2012, Kunder tweeted: 'I'll always regret one thing that I feel guilty about. I sincerely apologise for my tweet on *Ra.One* @iamsrk.' Farah supported her husband and was quoted saying: 'I'm proud of my husband. It takes a big heart to apologise.'

A truce between the two parties was initiated by friends and eventually Farah again directed Shah Rukh for *Happy New Year*, but unlike her previous films with Shah Rukh, this time the editor of her film was not Kunder.

While the two volatile Khans had their fair share of uneasy turbulence, the other Khan, Aamir, kept off this path of explosive eruption. One cannot, however, obliterate his peaceful, but firm decision to boycott all Indian award shows, as he felt that the deserving did not always lift the award.

Aamir was not a member of the Angry Pathan Club, but in 1994, he co-starred with one of them, to make a film in their '*apna andaz*' (own style). A rip-roaring comedy that would go down to become a benchmark in Bollywood chronicles.

Kunder remains unclear', *The Times of India*, 31 Jan 2012, accessed May 2019, https://timesofindia.indiatimes.com/entertainment/hindi/bollywood/news/Why-Shah-Rukh-Khan-slapped-Farah-Khans-husband-Shirish-Kunder-remains-unclear/articleshow/11692530.cms

KHANtastic

10

Working Together: The Khans' Chemistry

*R*eally wonder how the film got made. No one was talking to anyone. Aamir played maximum pranks, Salman did awesome scenes, also gave many *gaalis* (abuses), Lolo (Karisma Kapoor) and I sulked! Raj (the director Rajkumar Santoshi) was hilarious and also in love, and the producer was broke.'

These are excerpts from Raveena Tandon's tweet on twenty-four years since the release of *Andaz Apna Apna*.

The three Khans have been seen in pairs in seven films together, but Aamir and Salman have co-starred in only one film. The boys were already romantic icons at that time but this rib-tickling comedy, which had these heroes playing comedians, was quirky as well as extremely risky for them.

Those days, post the super success of *Ghayal* in 1990, Rajkumar Santoshi was a sought-after director, while the producer Vinay Sinha (who used to be *Sholay* villain Amjad Khan's secretary) was well connected in the industry. Sinha told Santoshi that he already had Aamir on board and that he had spoken to Salim Khan, who had confirmed that Salman would be ready too. All he needed was a director and a story to get cracking. Santoshi too wanted to clinch the project, but the hitch was that there was no story and no script. There was only a germ of a unique thought.

In the early 1990s, Salman was busy doing many projects and every film would be infamous for his changing hairstyles. *Andaz Apna Apna* took a couple of years to be made, so in many scenes, he had long hair from his *Saajan* days, while in some scenes, he had short hair from his *Hum Aapke Hain Koun..!* continuity. The vibe was that he was an impromptu actor. While he would not be a part of story sessions and other technical aspects of the film, he would come to the set and set it on fire with his natural and extempore performance.

Aamir, on the other hand, did select work at that time too. He was only committed to one film at a time. So, he became part of the story sessions and contributed to the growth of the script. A lot of the film was constructed on gut and impromptu decisions. For instance, when the unit reached the studio to shoot the climax, it was just an empty space and they had no clue what to shoot, so they sat to plan at the location. What finally showed up onscreen was super hit with the audience.

Raveena was already working with Salman and Lateef Binny, Santoshi's chief assistant director, knew Karisma's mother, Babita. Thus, both Raveena and Karisma were signed up.

The mahurat of the film was held at Sun-n-Sand Hotel where noted filmstar Dharmendra gave the clap. It was attended by many Bollywood celebrities and even cricketing legend Sachin Tendulkar was present at the event. The first shot began with Aamir and Salman having a tiff in front of a Hanuman Mandir, and thus started a journey, which ironically would be full of such tiffs and pranks.

The roller-coaster ride of making the film took over three years with continuous changes in the script and scenes. The scenes had to be written, improvised and rewritten on the sets. Dates had to be adjusted with artist availability and if this was not stressful in itself, there were financial hiccups too. The film well overshot its estimated time of making, thus being compared to the never-ending cult-classic, *Mughal-E-Azam*, which too was eternally in the making.

Cult Status

Despite the turbulent journey of the making of the film, Sinha recalls that whenever he took his family to the set to watch the shoot, his children would fall off their seats laughing while watching the scenes. Once the cameras rolled, both Aamir and Salman were a riot together. On camera and off it, while performing funny scenes, they would often break into uncontrollable laughter and at times, it would carry on for hours.

What happened behind the scenes was no less funny. The biggest prankster on the set was none other than Aamir. Raveena was then friends with Salman, as they had already worked in a film, but for *Andaz Apna Apna*, she was paired opposite Aamir, who was new to her. She had no idea what Aamir was capable of.

They were shooting on this moving tonga, and Raveena was brushing her hair, when Aamir came with a cup of tea, asking, 'Ravs, *tu chai peeyegi*? (Ravs, will you have some tea?)' Before she could answer, he dropped the cup and saucer on her. She shrieked thinking piping hot tea had fallen on her and Aamir burst out laughing. He had actually tied an empty cup with the saucer to give an impression that it had tea in it.

Raveena, too, decided to get even with him and it was with the help of none other than choreographer, Saroj Khan. Aamir was in the washroom and it was time to pack up, when

Raveena suddenly had an idea. Taking Saroj into confidence to hatch a plan, she requested the dance director to give Aamir a very complicated dance step and to tell him that this had to be filmed immediately.

When Aamir returned to the shoot, a poker-faced Saroj went as per the plan. Aamir was a bit taken aback at this sudden change of schedule and the intricacy of the near-impossible dance move, but he readily agreed to do it and called Raveena to practise with him. The choreographer stepped in, telling him that Raveena had already picked up the step in Aamir's absence, so it was only Aamir who had to put in the legwork. For a long while Aamir practised the step. A lot of the unit had dispersed by then, but so intense was Aamir's attention to his work that he did not pay heed to the reducing number of people on the set. Once he was finally able to pick up the step, he was told that the same would have to be performed on top of a tonga.

Initially horrified, an unsuspecting Aamir followed the ace choreographer's instructions and boarded the top of the tonga. Raveena was hysterical and was trying her best to conceal her laughter. Ishwar Bidri, the cinematographer, who had been roped in too, followed the plan and rolled the camera on cue. Aamir began performing on the tonga with full dedication as onlookers controlled their giggles for a while and then convulsed into an explosive bout of laughter. And Raveena screamed out loudly, 'We fooled you!' Aamir realized the prank and smiled sheepishly.

Another time, during a schedule in Panchgani, in Maharashtra, the filming had to be stopped. The unit had no permission to extend the shoot and was running short of funds. Aamir, who was very involved in the project, stepped in.

He bailed out the unit by paying ₹5,000 from his own pocket so that the film could be shot at the location for which they neither had permission nor funds.

However, every memorable episode was not that of laughter and innocent mirth. Sometimes bitterness crept in when Salman felt that Aamir was being favoured as the director spent more time with him. Binny, the film's chief assistant director, helped clear the air and explained to Salman that it was so because Aamir did a lot of rehearsals while Salman didn't. Aamir was prepared and Salman was spontaneous.

The fact that Aamir spent a lot of time at edit also irked Salman, but soon he realized that both had a fair division of screen time. In the film, Aamir was the over-smart friend, while Salman was the simpleton. Initially, two major scenes were written in a way where Aamir would outsmart Salman but later, on Aamir's counsel, it was changed. Aamir felt that both actors were of equal importance and should have scenes of foremanship over one another for the audience to identify with the leads and enjoy the show.

Yet, there were instances of harsh confrontations and hurtful memories that created unbridgeable cracks. One such ego issue that transpired was between the two superstars, though not directly. The shooting of the song 'Yeh raat aur yeh doori' stretched over a bit of time and everyone's patience was dwindling. Salman was seething as he felt Saroj Khan had reserved the best steps for Aamir and after the shoot, he had a huge confrontation with the choreographer, accusing her for being unfair to him.

The master dance director recalls that those were the days when Salman did not have rhythm nor was he a dancer. So following the dholki (a two-headed drum) rhythm of the song and the director's brief, Saroj had laid out her plans fairly. She was simply doing what her director had asked her to do and what worked for the overall song.

But when Salman walked up to her and said, '*Tum Aamir Khan ke g***d mein bahut ghusti ho na? Mai jab hero ban jaunga, aur top ka hounga, tab main tumhare saath toh kaam nahi karunga.* Let's shake hands (You are biased towards Aamir. So, when I become a big star I will never work with you)'. This created a rift between the two of them and they never worked together again.

Even Raveena and Karisma, during those days, had a tiff and were not talking to each other. Photojournalist Pradeep Bednekar, recalls their rift with a funny incident. Throughout the film, the girls refused to pose alongside each other. But in the climactic scene when the two girls were tied to a pole, they couldn't avoid each other's company. That was the time Bednekar went on a clicking spree and was able to click numerous images of the two together.

Everyone from the unit remembers that Aamir was most sincere and punctual of the young bandwagon. For a 9 a.m. shift at Madh Island, he would reach an hour early, even though he stayed in Khar, which was almost 25 km away. Not only that, he would be ready with make-up and his lines too. Salman, working many shifts and many movies at that time, was a different story. There were days when he would miss his call time by a big margin.

The film's chief assistant director, Binny, recalls that day when they were shooting at Madh Island, and as per routine, the unit was ready, but there was no sign of Salman. Binny called Salman's home and his mother picked up the landline. Binny requested her to wake up Salman. She said she had tried hard but wasn't able to stir the sleeping Khan. She asked Binny to come over and wake him up. Binny reached Salman's house near Bandstand after a long one-hour drive. Then he, along with some unit hands, hoisted the sleeping Salman and hauled him into the car. Throughout the entire ride back to Madh Island, Salman remained fast asleep in the car. A quick shave was given to the sleeping Salman in the make-up room before he was woken up and readied to face the camera.

This film paid tribute to a lot of real-life incidents and other films too. Some immensely memorable ones were when Salman is asked whether he has seen *Sholay* and he says, '*Haan, dus baar* (Yes, ten times),' to which Aamir retorts, '*Iske baap ne hi toh likhi hai* (It is his father who has written it).' The pun was on the fact that it was Salman's father, Salim Khan, who was actually the co-writer of the blockbuster *Sholay*. In another scene, Salman hums the immensely popular 'Dekha hai pehli baar' song from his previous hit *Saajan*.

Aamir had his equitable share of stardom references in the film. The scene in which Aamir cuts a ribbon, 'Papa kehte hai bada naam karega,' his introductory song from *Qayamat Se Qayamat Tak*, is played in the background. And in a first, Aamir made a special appearance in Santoshi's film *Damini*, and in a scene said that he was working on a film called *Andaz Apna Apna*.

While on a promotional tour to Canada, where Salman and Aamir were performing together, Salman said that Aamir and he shared fan attention jointly and it was all teamwork. In this light-hearted interview, he impersonated Aamir and confused the interviewer but later summed it up by saying that Aamir has put in an incredible performance in the film. Aamir too went on record saying, 'Salman had done one of his best works in *Andaz Apna Apna*.' Truer words were never spoken.

When released, the film met with a lukewarm response at the box office but is one of those exceptional features that rose above box-office figures and today has reached cult status.

A sequel to this comical craze has been in news for some time but without any concrete announcement of a production. Commenting on this, Raveena had said:[33]

> I would love to be game for it, but I know that my photograph is going to be hanging there. Aamir and Salman will be garlanding Lolo (Karisma Kapoor) and me, and saying *'hamaari biwiyaan mar gayi, ab kya karein*? [our wives are dead, what do we do now?]' And then they will be running after 21-year-old heroines. So that's how the sequel is gonna start.

Around the early 1990s, when the two Bandra Boys were sharing screen space in *Andaz Apna Apna*, two interesting things happened. Director Yash Chopra offered a film to Aamir that he rejected. And Salman was offered a film by the music label, Venus, that he too let go.

The outsider Khan from Delhi accepted both these offers. Throwing caution to the wind, with these two unconventional choices that were rejected by his contemporaries, he was right on his mark to create history.

---

[33]*India Today* Web Desk, 'Raveena Tandon's dig at Salman and Aamir: They will run after twenty-one-year-old heroines', *India Today*, 19 April 2017, accessed September 2019, https://www.indiatoday.in/movies/gossip/story/raveena-tandon-salman-aamir-khan-andaz-apna-apna-sequel-972271-2017-04-19

11

The Great Gambler

After having arrived from Delhi, the young actor from TAG was strengthening his foothold in Bombay. He had made his big-screen debut with a film rejected by another actor. Armaan Kohli[34] had shot for a few days and had then walked out of *Deewana*.

Shah Rukh played the role of a second hero in the love triangle *Deewana*, with Rishi Kapoor in the lead, and the film turned out to be a blockbuster. Shah Rukh went on to lift the Filmfare Best Male Debut award (1992–93). The award show had an emotional Shah Rukh raising his trophy to the skies and saying, 'Mom, this one is for you.' The world had started to notice him.

Shah Rukh was unpredictable. He did not follow a formula. He was a volcano of emotions, waiting to erupt. He didn't mind daring rejects. 'I never listen to scripts. I listen to the heartbeat of the film-maker,' he once stated.

Around this time, Abbas and Mustan Burmawalla (more popularly known as Abbas–Mustan), the director siblings who had hit the bullseye with their suspense thriller *Khiladi*, were

---

[34]The son of film director Rajkumar Kohli and actress Nishi, Armaan Kohli made his debut in his father's 1992 film *Virodhi*. He was to star in *Deewana* opposite Divya Bharti but walked out of the film after shooting for the first schedule. Shah Rukh replaced him in *Deewana*, which turned out to be a blockbuster.

ready to launch their next. The film was inspired by a single scene in a Hollywood film, *A Kiss Before Dying*, that sent chills down the duo's spine. In this film, the hero, while having a romantic conversation with his girlfriend, throws her off a terrace, killing her. This scene left such an impression on the directors that they wrote a film script to incorporate the scene. It was titled *Baazigar*.

The directors aspired to cast the top young Khans, Aamir and Salman, but unfortunately for them the script did not create a stir amongst the A-list actors.

Aamir could not identify with the character and let it pass. When Abbas–Mustan approached Salman, the actor asked Salim Khan for his inputs. The veteran writer felt that as it was a story about a negative character, they should add an angle of the protagonist's mother to get the audience's sympathy for the hero. The directors did not agree and Salman didn't come on board. Much later, Salman said, 'When I turned down the film, they went to Shah Rukh and then they added the mother angle!'

Anil Kapoor was the next one to reject the film because of the negative lead character. The directors panicked and went to the last remaining Khan. Shah Rukh was then a minor player in the industry and producer Ratan Jain, of Venus Records and Tapes, was not sure about casting him in the lead for *Baazigar*.

Shah Rukh had come to their office for another script narration, where he met the director duo by chance. The directors found something extremely striking in this Delhi boy's aura, and they realized that he was the only one willing to gamble with his image. It was a long narration of over an hour, and at the end of it, Shah Rukh loved the idea of playing the bad guy. He could empathize with the humanization of the villain. He was going to be the *Baazigar*.

With Shah Rukh on board, the producers wanted to reinforce the saleability of the project and hence, wanted to cast big names such as Sridevi or Juhi Chawla in the lead. The directors felt differently. The Burmawallas were sure that only a fresh pairing would be apt for the film. They approached Kajol, who was then one-film old. *Bekhudi* had not created much of a stir, but Kajol had been noticed for her performance. Mustan recalls, 'When we went to meet Kajol, she was so lively and jovial, we felt she might not be able to understand the script and her role. But she showed maturity and remained focused.' Shilpa Shetty was the other heroine who was paired opposite Shah Rukh, and it was her debut.

Thanks to Salim Khan, now the crux of the plot lay in the emotional pulse of the mother-son angle and Rakhee Gulzar, who had been loved as the mother in *Ram Lakhan*, was the ideal choice to play the distressed lady. She readily agreed.

With a fresh pair of girls and a television star in the lead who had just played second lead to Rishi Kapoor, *Baazigar* rolled in December 1992. But the shoot hit a roadblock almost immediately. Babri Masjid had just been demolished and there were widespread riots all over the country. Tension had seeped into the film industry and majority of work was stalled due the hostile atmosphere of large-scale protests that followed the riots in Bombay after the Masjid demolition.

Four months later, in March 1993, the film rolled again and Abbas–Mustan heaved a sigh of relief. However, they were not prepared for the phenomenon—Shah Rukh Khan.

During fight scenes, it was common practice that directors and fight masters tried their best to cheat the blow, so no one is harmed. Shah Rukh would not settle for that. Dalip Tahil, who had played Aamir's father in *Qayamat Se Qayamat Tak* and was now playing the antagonist, and Shah Rukh's father-in-law, in *Baazigar*, recalls a tricky incident at the shoot.

In a scene, Tahil was required to slap Shah Rukh hard. Abbas–Mustan, as per protocol, directed Tahil to cheat the blow, so as not to hurt Shah Rukh. But Shah Rukh assured the directors all would go well and then took Tahil aside. He told him, '*Muhjhe jitna chaho thapad laga lo. Bas, scene kamaal ki honi chahiye* (Slap me as much as you want. The scene should turn out perfectly).' The scene remains one of the most memorable high points of the film.

Shah Rukh wasn't afraid of not looking good in his close-ups. He was happy with blood streaming down his bashed-up face and would prod the directors to shoot one scene with four to five variations, till they were satisfied. For the scene in which he kills Shilpa Shetty's friend (played by Resham Tipnis), Shah Rukh suggested he should tear her photo and put it in his mouth rather than keeping it in his pocket. It was one of the most dramatic and talked-about scenes in the film.

The film was not only about drama and intensity. The young unit did not miss a chance to have fun at the shoot as well. The action scenes with the sports cars had the gizmo-freak child in Shah Rukh all excited. The *Fauji* boy loved his cars. He drove all the sports cars that had come to the shoot and had a terrific time shooting this scene.

Shah Rukh went beyond being just an actor on the sets. For *Baazigar*, he helped acquire permissions for the shoot, especially in his hometown, Delhi. This habit of his carried on to the sets of *Kabhi Haan Kabhi Naa* too, where, when the production ran out of film stock in a late-night shift, Shah Rukh went to every shooting unit at Kamalistan Studio to ask for fresh stock, so that he could give a better take for his incomplete shot. When he failed to get it, he sat and wailed in despair.

Not only Abbas–Mustan but even his leading ladies, Shilpa Shetty and Kajol, were all praises for Shah Rukh's camaraderie and sharp filmmaking intelligence. Shilpa says, 'He was supportive. I remember when we were shooting the 'Aye mere humsafar' song in *Baazigar*, he told me that the camera is the audience. To date, I keep that in mind when I'm giving a shot. Working with him was a learning experience.' Kajol, who went on to become an iconic hit pair with Shah Rukh, says, 'I've never met a more hard-working man than Shah Rukh. He sleeps for three hours and wakes up thinking about what all he needs to do. There aren't enough hours in a day for him. People overlook the fact that he has worked hard to reach where he is. It takes more than just luck to achieve so much.'

And then, one day, while shooting *Baazigar*, Shah Rukh, along with Vivek Vaswani, was watching *Lamhe*, when his secretary, Anwar, called and said, 'Yashji is making a film. He has thought of casting you and he will be calling you.' Shah Rukh immediately left the movie midway and eagerly waited for the phone call.

No Guts, No Story: Celebrating the Anti-hero

Yash Chopra, possibly India's most successful director of romantic films, was planning to make a thriller. It had started with Uday Chopra, Yash Chopra's younger son, and his young friend, Hrithik Roshan, forcing Aditya Chopra, Uday's elder brother, to watch an Australian thriller called *Dead Calm*.

The film remained stuck in Aditya's head and he conceived a low-budget, dark film about an obsessive lover who terrorises a married couple on a ship. There were to be no songs in the film. The name of the film was also inspired from Hrithik's amateur short film, *Darr*, which he had directed.

The story was first narrated to Rishi Kapoor for the lead. Though he did not do the film, he did suggest that Yash Chopra himself direct it as a big-budget presentation in true-blue Yash Chopra style.

Yash Chopra launched *Darr* but found it extremely challenging to cast the second lead, the role of the mentally disturbed lover, Rahul Mehra. He had asked actors like Sanjay Dutt and Ajay Devgn to take up the role, but all had turned him down. Finally, Aamir said yes to the film.

But Aamir had a condition. He wanted a joint narration with the lead of the film, Sunny Deol. Yash Chopra was fine with it at first but later changed his mind. When Aamir persisted, the director called him and said, 'Aamir, let's work some other time.' The actor immediately said, 'Fine.' He later said that he wanted to be sure of two things when he took on a role. One, that the film would work with the audience. And two, that he would enjoy playing the role. As Aamir elaborated later, 'My doubts about enjoying the film surfaced when the director refused to give a joint narration. In a way, I was relieved when I was finally out of the film because this was better than suffering all through its shooting. If I felt sad, it was for missing on a good role.' Later, he added, 'I will never ever work with Yash Chopra. Our styles of working are different.'

Finally, Rishi Kapoor came to Yash Chopra's rescue and told him that his young co-star in *Deewana* would be able to do the negative character justice. Aditya had loved Shah Rukh's performance in *Deewana*. Though he felt the performance was over the top, he could identify with the intelligent actor within Shah Rukh. Yash Chopra, however, did not find Shah Rukh to be his idea of a hero, but since the role had been rejected by several actors, he did not have much of a choice but to make that fateful call to Shah Rukh.

Yash Chopra was Shah Rukh's dream director and the passionate actor was not going to say no under any circumstance. And along with *Baazigar*, this was Shah Rukh's second film as a psychotic anti-hero.

Even after the Chopras cast Shah Rukh for *Darr*, they kept feeling bad about having lost out on Aamir. But only till Shah Rukh arrived on the sets. His first scene in the film was when he secretly gatecrashed into the heroine, Kiran's (Juhi Chawla) Holi party. As he watched her flirt with colours with her husband, Lieutenant Commander Sunil Malhotra (Sunny Deol), he went into a crazy frenzy, beating the drums. Shah Rukh's energy and expression had his relationship sealed with Yash Chopra for good. Shah Rukh became Chopra's Rahul Mehra and in subsequent years, a habit with the director. After *Darr*, Chopra never directed a film without Shah Rukh in it.

The climactic scene of *Darr* had deterred many heroes from playing the part, as they did not want to be beaten up by another star. But Shah Rukh let Sunny thrash him, as he probably knew that he would run away with the audience's sympathy. At the shoot, Sunny realized the film was slipping out of his hands. In the scene where Shah Rukh was to stab Sunny, the Deol debated with Yash Chopra, that he being a fit and athletic commando would be too sharp to let Shah Rukh overpower him in this fashion. But Chopra stuck to his belief and a furious Sunny stuffed his hands into his trousers pockets and ripped them off in contained anger. Later, Sunny accused Shah Rukh of manipulating the script to win the viewers' sympathy and did not speak to him for sixteen-long years. He never ever worked with Yash Chopra again.

Baazigar was to release on 12 November 1993, followed by *Darr* on 24 December. Venus organized a travelling premiere. The crew went to several theatres on the opening night, mingling with the crowds and taking in reactions. There was a stunned silence during the murder scenes and a deafening applause was heard when Shah Rukh exacted the final bloody revenge in *Baazigar*. When the actor threw Shilpa Shetty from the terrace, the audience simply loved it. And the whistling never stopped when he delivered the now famous dialogue, *'Kabhi kabhi kuch jeetne ke liye, kuch harna padta hai, aur haar ke jeetne wale ko Baazigar kehte hain* (Sometimes to win something, you let go of something else, and that is the trait of a gambler)*.'*

The overseas distributor, Eros International, had organized six premieres over three days in the United Kingdom. Shah Rukh and Gauri were in their London hotel, when producer Yash Johar called them at the crack of dawn with news from India. *Baazigar* was not a hit. It was a super hit! *Darr* followed in Christmas and received the same fate. It was raining hits for Shah Rukh.

When asked about his choice of these two films, Shah Rukh had said, 'I had no misconception that I could be a hero. Maybe that's why I did anti-hero roles, which others refused. I did not have any qualms about the character being good or bad, I just wanted to act. I still do, whenever I get an opportunity. It's my core, and what I love doing most, and what I want to die doing.'

And what he loved doing most, got him nominations for three Filmfare awards that year—Best Actor for *Baazigar*, Best Villain for *Darr* and Critics Award (Best Actor) for *Kabhi Haan Kabhi Naa*. *Baazigar* swept the awards and so did Shah Rukh. While receiving it, he said, 'I hope I keep coming back.'

As Shah Rukh lifted the Black Lady for his first Best Actor award in the viewers' choice category, in 1994, he looked around for his directors, Abbas and Mustan, who were conspicuous by their absence at the function. He decided that he could not go home with the award without meeting the men-in-white who had made it possible for him. He found out where his directors lived, and despite the late hour, he decided to drop in.

Abbas–Mustan lived in South Bombay's Bhendi Bazaar. Shah Rukh met the brothers and told them that he had to take their blessings. He touched their feet to show his respect and then celebrated with them. When Shah Rukh headed out of their house, it was almost dawn. It was the month of Ramadan and the people of Bhendi Bazaar had woken up before sunrise to eat their suhūr (pre-dawn meal). The news that Shah Rukh Khan was in the locality spread like wildfire. People from the locality thronged to see the new, emerging star. An emotional Shah Rukh had tears in his eyes.

'No guts, no story' was what the mettlesome Shah Rukh believed. He had signed up two projects rejected by the two Bandra Boys—Salman and Aamir. This ticking bomb of live energy had shot the two films together, and sometimes on the same day in different shifts. The results had finally paid off. So aptly, in January 1994, *Filmfare* put him on their cover and captioned it 'The Great Gambler'.

'The Outsider' was here to stay.

Sanjukta Nandy

12

Aamir Khan: The Perfect Superstar

*A*amir Khan became a star overnight. Much sought after, following the success of *Qayamat Se Qayamat Tak*, Aamir hurriedly signed about ten films in a row—a norm those days with successful actors. Unfortunately, these films were not turning out to his satisfaction. Aamir would be so unhappy shooting them that he would return home after pack-up and weep. Once these films released, his worst fears were confirmed. The films started to flop, one after another. *Raakh*, *Love Love Love* and *Tum Mere Ho* were three flops in a row. The pressure to prove himself was tremendous. That's when the whispers began to do the rounds: Aamir was another Kumar Gaurav. Just a one-film wonder. It was all over for him.

Unhappy with the quality of work he was doing, Aamir decided to stop compromising with his roles and choose his scripts more carefully. He decided to do a film only if he had conviction in the script, and that would be the sole driving force.

That's when Mahesh Bhatt came to him with a film. Bhatt was a successful director of that time and at the top of his game. Aamir was very excited. He knew that an association with Bhatt would resurrect his career that was slipping into a cesspool of quick failure. But when the director narrated the story to Aamir, he was disappointed and faced a dilemma: the desire of an association with Bhatt but with a script that he did not like. Unable to speak his mind to Bhatt, Aamir requested for twenty-four hours to take a decision.

Aamir went back to Bhatt the next day and said that he would not be able to do the film. It was not a story that excited him. 'Had I not kept the promise I had made to myself or compromised with my core belief, I would have been doing different films today,' says Aamir.

Meanwhile, in the late 1980s, a film called *Khunda*, starring Shashi Kapoor, Danny Denzongpa, Rohan Kapoor, Farha Naaz and Tabu was announced. The film was to be directed by Chandra Barot (of *Don* fame). Suddenly the film changed hands and a debutant director came on board. The director, Indra Kumar, approached Aamir to star in it. The script revolved around Raja, who lives with his poor parents, but attends college where he has several run-ins with other wealthy collegians. Later, when a fellow collegian accuses Raja of sexual molestation, Raja's father seizes the opportunity, masquerades as a wealthy businessman and approaches the girl's father to arrange for their children to get married. Aamir thought that the film had a novel concept and could be path-breaking. The rest is history.

The film, now with a new title, *Dil*, had its fair share of trials with a new director and a hiccupping flow of funds. But none of it was as tough as handling the unbelievable pranks Aamir played on the sets, specially, with his leading lady, Madhuri Dixit. One day at the shoot, Aamir and Madhuri were sitting together and Aamir was reading Madhuri's palm. Indra Kumar joined in and heard Aamir saying, 'One day you will become a very big heroine. You will be a superstar.' Though he knew

Aamir was no palm reader, Kumar made the mistake of joining in to support the story. He was completely unaware of what Aamir would do next. While Madhuri listened raptly, Aamir caught her unaware and spat right into her palm.

Madhuri couldn't believe what Aamir had done. Filled with rage, she ran after him to slap him and a chase ensued, with them running in the auditorium where they were shooting for the song 'Khambe jaisi khadi hai'. When she couldn't catch him, she fired Kumar, who she thought was a willing accomplice. The poor director did not know what had hit him. Aamir later made peace with Madhuri, but she remained eternally cautious of him.

A brazen prankster on the sets, Aamir was a different person in front of the camera, forever evolving and completely dedicated to the director. Aamir's role in *Dil* had many shades to it and he rose to the occasion to fulfill every facet of romance, intensity, comedy, dance and drama to bring alive the role of Raja in the film. This was done with painstaking rehearsals and a lot of sweat. After a series of flops, it was Aamir's litmus test.

On its release, *Dil* made its way to the top of the box-office chart, emerging as the highest grosser of 1990. The film marked Aamir's evolution as an actor. He brought alive a character, very different from his chocolate-boy image and a far cry from his own true persona. Later, Aamir said, 'When *Dil* worked well, it gave me a new lease of life. It gave me the power to begin again.' However, Aamir's performance that year in the Best Actor category was overlooked at the Filmfare Awards (1991), while Madhuri won her first Filmfare Best Actress award for *Dil*. Just as this film launched Aamir's upward graph in the industry, it also sowed the seeds of his strained relationship with Indian film awards.

After *Dil*'s success, Mahesh Bhatt approached Aamir once again for a new film. This time Aamir said yes. The film's leading lady was Bhatt's daughter, Pooja, the Lux Fresh Face (now known as the Best Female Debut) of 1990, and the film was inspired from the 1934 Hollywood film, *It Happened One Night*. The film titled *Dil Hai Ki Manta Nahin* was a romantic comedy about Pooja Dharamchand (Pooja Bhatt), a spoilt runaway heiress in search of her movie star boyfriend who eventually falls in love with Raghu Jetley (Aamir), a newspaper reporter who offers her safe passage to Bombay.

Pooja remembers fighting with Aamir throughout the making of the film. She recalls, 'Aamir and I were magic on screen and a disaster off it. He was my favourite sparring partner. "Tom and Jerry" is how Uncle Mukesh (Bhatt) described us. We were as different as chalk and cheese, and that's why our chemistry was so palpable on screen.'

Aamir was meticulous and worked hard for this film which was painstakingly made. Aamir's co-star, Tiku Talsania, remembers the day when Aamir was shooting for the song, 'Tu pyaar hai kisi aur ka'. Aamir was very nervous. It was an emotional scene in which he would have to bring out restrain as well as drama. He wanted the emotions to come across as real and was trying to work it out in his head. Before attempting a difficult shot, a stressed Aamir took some time out to play with glass marbles, working to get his aim right. This helped to increase his concentration, calmed him down and interestingly this technique worked bang on, every time.

Aamir developed a good comradeship with Tiku while working on the film and it was a happy goodbye once the shoot was wrapped up. But suddenly, one day Tiku got a call from Mahesh Bhatt, who requested him to come over to Film

City as Aamir wanted to reshoot a scene. Tiku hurried to the location, only to see Aamir waiting at the gate for him. He knew Aamir had something to say and feared it was not going to be very palatable.

Those days, it was well known that often stars felt challenged by performances of co-stars and hence, would have their parts chopped. When Aamir revealed that they would need to reshoot a particular scene, Tiku dreaded that the same fate awaited him too. But when he asked Aamir the reason for the reshoot, the actor explained that his character, Raghu, was so full of self-pride in the film that he had not taken financial help from his father. So, when in one scene, he takes financial aid from his newspaper editor and boss, played by Tiku, Aamir felt this would not gel with the core essence of the character and hence, convinced Bhatt to reshoot the scene. The meticulous Khan had seen the film twenty-seven times before reaching this conclusion. They reshot the scene and it went on to become one of the most remarkable and memorable scenes in the film.

Dil Hai Ke Manta Nahin took Aamir's career to the next level. In an interview to *Filmfare* (1991), he had said, 'This film was different. It is one film which I've enjoyed working in and I've liked the result when I finally saw it. So it was very important to me that people liked it. And I'm glad that they have.'

Aamir was diligent and meticulously involved in not only the moves of the character in a scene but with every bit of constructing Raghu into a distinctive and believable character. He even chose the name. He liked the ring to Raghu Jetley, as he felt it resonated with the character who was not instantly likable and had several layers to his personality. Aamir spent

119

hours on the character's costumes; a lot of it were used clothes, shoes, watches and specially the white cap that became a rage after the film. The decision to give the cap to the character was discussed for hours by Aamir and the creative team. Aamir's patent approach was to discuss things endlessly, because he believed that unless he pondered over something, he wasn't giving his 100 per cent to it.

The same rigour Aamir carried into his next role in *Jo Jeeta Wohi Sikandar* (1992), which was director Mansoor Khan's follow-up on *Qayamat Se Qayamat Tak*. This film, rooted in a realistic social situation, was a far cry from the stereotypical flavour of the 1990s. It portrayed the rivalry between local schools especially a rich arrogant boy (Deepak Tijori) and a poor one (Aamir), also a prankster who runs a small café, which culminates in the biggest annual school cycling event. Undaunted by the novel theme, Aamir trusted his gut feeling and supported Mansoor once again. The media called it the 'break away' film that broke the set pattern of storytelling and was also inspired by the 1979 American film *Breaking Away*. *Jo Jeeta Wohi Sikandar* went on to win the Filmfare Award for Best Film, surpassing that year's blockbuster, *Beta*. But Aamir once again lost the Best Actor award, this time to Anil Kapoor for *Beta*.

Following the success of *Jo Jeeta Wohi Sikandar*, Aamir stepped into *Hum Hain Rahi Pyar Ke*, again directed by Mahesh Bhatt, who had already delivered a hit with Aamir. But for Aamir what mattered was only the honesty of the script and that's what he saw in this film. Here, he shared screen space with his *Qayamat Se Qayamat Tak* heroine, Juhi Chawla and a bunch of children, who kept playing pranks on him throughout the film. In the film, Aamir played Rahul Malhotra, the manager of the family's heavily-in-debt garments business. He is also the guardian of his dead sister's three mischievous kids for whom he hires Vyjayanti (Juhi Chawla) as governess, who has run away from her orthodox family.

Only a self-assured actor like Aamir could share the screen with so many actors without being intimidated by them. *Hum Hain Rahi Pyar Ke*, inspired by the 1958 Hollywood film, *Houseboat*, met with conscientious detailing from Aamir and was turned around to become a film that emerged with its own unique identity. For instance, in one particular scene, his character, Rahul Malhotra, had a target of delivering 700 shirts on a steep deadline. Not enough junior artists were present on the day of the shoot. His co-star, Tiku Talsania, remembers that Aamir was not only sharp enough to point out this anomaly on the sets but also recollected that the previous scene in which the order for the shirts had been taken, had more junior artists. Aamir's logic was that why would the workers lessen in number once the order was taken? Aamir stopped the shoot and insisted that all the junior artists be called for the shoot to maintain consistency and quality of the film. That day his father, and producer of the film, Tahir Hussain, was also present at the shoot. But Aamir stood his ground and Tahir saab finally caved in under his son's logic and firmness.

The shoot of the film was laced with agony and ecstasy. While it was not a tough job to handle the initially 'innocent' kids, as they got comfortable, they proved a match for Aamir, otherwise always the prankster. Before the children, Aamir suddenly graduated to 'Uncle mode', as it dawned on him that he would need to take a more serious avatar than he usually did at work. This was the only way to keep his sanity and take charge of the kids. In fact, the climax scene, in which the children throw eggs at the villains, was Aamir's idea. As the kids had thrown eggs at Bijlani (Dalip Tahil) and Maya (Navneet Nishan) in an earlier scene, Aamir thought that it could be used once again. He was right. The scene had the audience falling off their seats and was a mention in most rave reviews.

For Aamir, a stickler for perfection, the film meant everything. He was involved in every department and never lost focus. This perhaps led to simmering allegations that Aamir had ghost directed the film, something both Aamir and Mahesh Bhatt vehemently refuted in separate interviews.

No Entry for Filmfare

Hum Hain Rahi Pyar Ke went on to win the 39th Filmfare Award for Best Film. Juhi bagged the trophy for the Best Actress, but Aamir once again lost the Best Actor award. This time to Shah Rukh, for a film he had let go—*Baazigar*. Not clinching the Best Actor award from Filmfare was becoming some sort of a norm for Aamir, but this did not dampen the rise of his stardom's mercury. Aamir had well begun to consolidate his position with three consecutive hits and was increasingly gaining a reputation for being a versatile actor.

In *Filmfare*, 1993, in a rare combined interview of Aamir and Shah Rukh, the 'Baazigar' spoke of Aamir, saying, 'He's one of the finest actors we have, someone I expect to evolve like Amitabh Bachchan, Shashi Kapoor and Rishi Kapoor. Or, just as Tom Cruise today. But Aamir should never fall prey to his own image. I know he has no limitations...' Shah Rukh also went on to add, 'Aamir, I feel you should start playing someone else besides Aamir Khan. You're good for another six–seven years and you'll be remembered for ten more for your performances.'[35] Shah Rukh was wrong. Aamir went on for much more than six years and ten memorable performances. He still reigns.

However, Aamir's luck after three consecutive successes, began to wane. His next film, *Baazi*, coming close on the heels of the successful *Hum Hain Rahi Pyar Ke*, met with a lukewarm response. But before it registered, Aamir once again stormed the box office with his path-breaking performance as Munna in *Rangeela*.

Falling into a mould was not for Aamir. He always chose projects that he found challenging. In *Rangeela*, Mili's (Urmilla Matondkar) ambition of becoming a famous actor meets several hurdles when Raj Kamal (Jackie Shroff), a suave actor, and Munna (Aamir), her street-smart childhood friend, both fall in love with her. 'There was no second thought while accepting the role of Munna. I knew he was an out-and-out winner,' said Aamir, who approached this role too, with the same intensity.

His character, Munna, was meant to dress in worn-out clothes. Aamir did not want to buy new clothes and then have to pass them off as old. He was pondering on how to bring in some authenticity, when he noticed a spot boy wearing an attire that looked unique. 'Bingo!' thought Aamir. The spot boy was given a brand-new wardrobe, and Aamir created a special tapori (vagabond) look for this film, complete with a black cap, an unbuttoned shirt and a handkerchief tied around his neck.

Ram Gopal Varma, the director of *Rangeela*, says, he learnt the value of test-runs and random feedback from Aamir,

---

[35]Christina Daniels, *I'll Do It My Way: The Incredible Journey of Aamir Khan*, Om Books International, 2012

who constantly sought feedback from the people he trusted, especially his cousins, Nuzhat and Mansoor Khan. He would then take notes in a writing pad and act on the inputs.

With painstaking rehearsals and diving into the nuances of a fictitious character, Aamir gave himself fully to Munna, which was so far away from his real-life persona. *Rangeela* went on to become a roaring hit.

Rangeela picked up six Filmfare awards in 1996, but the Best Actor award that year, once again went to the other Khan who had by now swept the nation off its feet with his tagline, 'Come, fall in love'. It is believed that this did not go down well with the perfectionist Khan and he thought that the organizers were biased towards Shah Rukh. It is rumoured that Aamir even had a showdown with the editor of the *Filmfare* magazine. Aamir never graced any Indian film award ceremony ever again.

Aamir never stopped being the prankster, especially when the script demanded it. For *Ishq*, which was a fun film, there were pranks galore on the sets. A significant film of Aamir's career in the 1990s, it marked the coming together of many proven hit combinations, Indra Kumar, Juhi Chawla and Aamir, who had all worked together before. They were joined by Ajay Devgn and Kajol; then an upcoming pair. The film portrayed two wealthy businessmen, Harbans Lal Saxena (Dalip Tahil) and Ranjit Rai (Sadashiv Amrapurkar) who wanted their children Madhu Saxena (Juhi) and Ajay Rai (Ajay) to marry each other. However, Madhu falls in love with Raja (Aamir), a mechanic, while Ajay falls in love with Kajal (Kajol).

The film set was ripe for practical jokes. Ajay and Aamir together were the masterminds and Tahil was the target this time. Tahil, required to adorn a bald look, was debating on how to get started on it. Aamir recommended a hair cream to him and Ajay seconded it as a good option. After using it, Tahil discovered that he had been recommended a women's hair removal cream. The bald look did work but regaining his hair wasn't such an easy feat for the actor.

The film also saw the break-up of Aamir and Juhi's long-standing friendship. It was again one of Aamir's pranks, the same one for which he was chased by Madhuri on the sets of *Dil*. Aamir once again spat, this time on Juhi's palm, and this led to a huge showdown. Juhi and Aamir, who had become a hit pair with *Qayamat Se Qayamat Tak* and went on to become 4 a.m. friends, drifted apart. After this episode, they sat far away from each other at the shoot. They did not speak to each other for six-long years following this falling-out. Sadly, Aamir and Juhi never worked together in any film again.

A Brush with Death

From 1990 to 1997, Aamir had seven hits under his belt, his most notable one being *Ghulam* in 1998, where a young Rani Mukerji, who was only one-film old (with *Raja Ki Aayegi Baraat*), was paired opposite him. Aamir was a huge star and Rani, a newcomer. During the shooting of the song '*Aakhon se tune yeh kya keh diya*,' Rani would look down at Aamir's shoes. Aamir requested her to look at him, as the lyrics were about looking into each other's eyes. Later, Rani revealed that she was reluctant to do so because she feared that looking into Aamir's eyes would make her fall in love with him.

Ghulam's heart-stopping train sequence is etched in the public's mind even today and Vikram Bhatt, the director of the film, remembers Aamir's close encounter with death.

Initially, Bhatt had insisted that this life-threatening stunt be done through visual effects. But the adrenaline-pumped Khan wanted to have it close to real. Against severe opposition from the director, Aamir stuck to his guns, '*Arey main kar loonga* and it won't be a problem (I will do it easily).' The director gave in to his insistence. What happened next shook everyone up.

Aamir was to run towards the train and jump out of the way before the train could hit him. The train came faster than Aamir had anticipated as he kept on running, leaping off the tracks just in the nick of time. When the editing team checked the footage, they were shocked to see that Aamir had averted the speeding train by just twenty-four frames. He was one second close to death. Years later, Aamir has still stored those twenty-four frames as a memory of his encounter with death.

Ghulam won the Best Scene award at the 44th Filmfare Awards in 1999. Yet again, Aamir was ignored. But Aamir had already stopped attending this award function by then. The trophies did not matter to him anymore. What mattered was his audience. 'For me, the biggest award I can get is the audience loving my film. That is all the confirmation I am looking for,' said Aamir.

Aamir was soon becoming a brand that was akin to a good movie. '*Aamir Khan hai, toh film achchi hogi* (If Aamir's in the film, it has to be good)' was the reputation that he was gaining with the audience. Aamir in a film meant that people would throng ticket counters. Aamir was no longer just a star. He was a superstar.

There were only two other actors who could match up to Aamir in this race for the numero uno spot. The other two Khans, Salman and Shah Rukh, were on their momentum of ascent too.

13

Salman Khan:
The Sultan as Superstar

*A*amir had once said about Salman, 'In *Andaz Apna Apna,* I had a very bad experience of working with him. I did not like him. I found him rude and inconsiderate.' However, in the next breath, Aamir confessed, 'For me, to give a big success, I have to have a great script, a great director and each technician has to contribute fully for the film to come out well and to do well. But Salman doesn't need that yaar. He is just raw, brute, star power. He just comes, shakes his belt a couple of times, puts his goggles behind his shirt and everyone just goes bananas. I don't have that kind of stardom.'

Salman's stardom had a meteoric rise with *Maine Pyar Kiya.* But many believed that it was Sooraj Barjatya and Bhagyashree who got the bigger bite of the industry limelight rather than Salman because for a good number of months, Salman did not get any film offers. It was only when a worried Salim Khan requested G.P. Sippy to just announce a film with Salman, to create a buzz in the trade, that the tide turned. The outcome was however, unexpected.

Ramesh Taurani, who had launched Tips Industries, a music production company, read the announcement of Sippy's *Patthar Ke Phool* starring Salman, with interest. At that time, he was on the lookout to buy the rights for music of new films. The music of *Maine Pyar Kiya* had done very well and so he decided to buy the music rights of *Patthar Ke Phool*. He was unaware that it was only an announcement for a film that was not going to be made.

On the following Monday morning, his first call was to Sippy. Taurani introduced himself and expressed an eagerness to meet him. As soon as Sippy gave the nod, Taurani hopped over to Sippy's office with an offer. He put down the money for the music rights of *Patthar Ke Phool*.

This was a pleasant surprise. Once Taurani showed his interest and confidence in the project, Raveena Tandon, who had then been noticed in a few ad films, was signed on and the stillborn project came alive. There was no looking back for Salman. In February 1991, *Patthar Ke Phool* rocked the box office.

Go Straight and Turn Right

But the release of this film wasn't Salman's immediate release post *Maine Pyar Kiya*. Salman had always dreamed of being a writer like his father. The story idea of *Baaghi: a rebel for love* was credited to Salman although scripted by Javed Siddiqui. Though *Patthar Ke Phool* was signed first, Salman's film, *Baaghi*, with Nagma as the heroine—released in December 1990—was a runaway hit.

But before the release of these films, film director Saawan Kumar Tak had called his friend Salim Khan and asked, '*Salman kya kar raha hai*? (What is Salman doing?)'. Salim saab said, '*Kuch nahi...sofe pe letaa hai bekaar* (Nothing, he is just lazing away on the sofa).' Tak responded, '*Bhej dijiyega, mere paas*

(Send him to me).' Salman was at Tak's place within an hour. First, he went to the fridge, ate some fruits and then went to Tak and said, '*Aa gaya hoon* (I've come).' Tak looked at him for a while and asked, '*Film shuru kare*? (Should we start the film?)'

Tak had planned *Sanam Bewafa* with two villainous stalwarts, Danny Denzongpa and Pran. He wanted to cast a young boy for the romantic angle. Salman was ready and the film took off. Tak still fondly looks back and says the honest romance that Salman portrayed carried the film that proved to be a smash hit in January 1991.

The release of *Sanam Bewafa* was quickly followed by *Patthar Ke Phool* in February 1991. Three months, three films and Salman had scored a hat-trick of hits. In August 1991 came *Saajan* which too made it to the top of the charts, scorching box-office numbers. The music too was a runaway hit. Four hits after *Maine Pyar Kiya* and Salman was tagged as the Sensational Khan by the media.

Salman was an unstoppable hit machine. He was creating waves in the industry and was flooded by film offers. He was working double and even triple shifts that amounted to almost twenty-four hours of work every day. He mentioned in an interview, 'All I heard resonating in my head was "*light aa raha hai and light jaa raha hai* (Bring the lights, take them away)".'

Those days, there were no vanity vans, so Salman had to sleep in his car. Luckily, his dad had a Mercedes-Benz with a comfortable back seat. But Salman's driver, Laxman dada, who had aged by then, one day went up to him, gave him the car keys and called it a day. He left saying that if he continued to drive for Salman, and keep up with this maddening schedule, he would surely land up killing them all in a road accident. A new driver came in for Salman, who carried on the pace.

In spite of the sweat and hard work, some rude flops were waiting around the corner for Salman. He later confessed that he himself was responsible for it. He was eager to buy his own house. So to garner the funds, he signed films, without much forethought. Some of these were also signed in *'yaari dosti'* (friendships). Salim Khan remembers that many times Salman would tell him to say 'no' to a friend on his behalf. Salman could never refuse anyone and his friends would convince him on emotional grounds to agree. As luck would have it, those films kept bombing one after another. *Love, Suryavanshi, Ek Ladka Ek Ladki, Nishchaiy* and *Dil Tera Aashiq* were all back-to-back flops.

One day, late in the night, concerned about Salman, Salim saab gave him some blunt advice, 'If there is anybody, any man who can foul it all up for you, it's going to be you! God doesn't want it to happen, we, your family don't want it to happen, and your fans most certainly don't want that to happen. So, again, if there's "anybody" who can mess it all up, it's you!' It was a wake-up call for Salman. His father's words shook him up and grounded his focus. Both his brothers, Arbaaz and Sohail, supported their father's advice and told Salman, 'If anyone can kill Gabbar Singh from *Sholay*, it's Gabbar himself.' Salman became sharper, aware and motivated with his choices. He caught onto the vibes of professionalism and his father's golden words, 'In life, go "straight" and turn "right".'

Re-scripting Box-Office History

'Straight and right' was Sooraj Barjatya and Rajshri Productions with a film called *Hum Aapke Hain Koun..!* Sooraj and Salman had spun magic in 1989 with *Maine Pyar Kiya* and it was their next venture together. A film with no action, no negative characters and fourteen songs. The pitch for the film was that it had values, traditions and a spirit of sacrifice that lay deep within the heart of the average Indian. Salman was again named Prem, the same name he had donned in *Maine Pyar Kiya*. Before this film, people in the industry were scared to keep the name 'Prem' for a hero, as it reminded them of the villain, Prem Chopra. But when Sooraj and Salman joined hands, it was always a break from the mould.

When Salman and Sooraj made *Maine Pyar Kiya*, they cried at every poignant moment of their camaraderie. On the first day of *Hum Aapke Hain Koun..!* too, they both got emotional at the thought of teaming up together again, and wept.

The release of the film coincided with the declaration of 1994 by the United Nations General Assembly as 'The International Year of the Family'. This family film, which many called an extended wedding video, had a screen full of characters, generally having fun, singing and dancing.

Spanning over a year, a big part of the film was shot in Ooty and in studios in Mumbai, especially Filmistan. The character of Prem was modelled on Salman himself. Prem was fun and energetic, similar to what Salman was on the sets.

Himani Shivpuri, who had come from Delhi with a theatre background, recalls that it was her first commercial film. Her debut scene was with Salman, who used to improvise a lot on the sets. He took her by complete surprise in the first shot itself. The scene in which Pooja Choudhury (Renuka Shahane) delivers her baby boy had a celebratory mood. Salman raised the momentum of the scene to another level of jubilation by hoisting Himani in his arms, and dancing with her. Sooraj and

Himani were both flabbergasted, but the mood of the scene got an extra dose of impromptu cheer.

Salman's inherent naughtiness translated into a lovable character on celluloid. His childish unscripted improvisations worked wonders as did his complete dedication to the film. Salman, allergic to dog hair, had a cold throughout the film. But he did all the scenes admirably, carrying Tuffy, the adorable Spitz, in his lap whenever and wherever it was required.

All the naughty interactions were planned by Sooraj but executed with an extra edge by Salman. The way Salman dealt with his co-stars, the children and even the dog was tender and honest. Everyone at the shoot noticed this quality and applauded. Between shots, the entire cast would team up and play games to de-stress and enjoy. The actors lived their roles in real life and the family-feeling filtered into their persona, which later reflected on screen and in the success of the film.

The wrap up of the shoot was extremely emotional. When any actor called in his last shot, the production would strum up a background song to bid them farewell. It was a song from the film itself, 'Tum se judaa ho kar, hume door jana hai (I will have to bid you adieu and go far from you).' This gesture made each of the actors, who gave their last shot, emotional. When it was Salman's time to bide farewell, Salman and Sooraj kept up their tradition of crying and wept once again.

In a few months, it was time for the audience to cry. The emotional joyride swept the nation on 5 August 1994. The theatre, Liberty, in Bombay, was decorated like a wedding set with lighting and flowers all over. Rajshri Productions was a famous distributor itself and went ahead with a new path-breaking release plan for the film. They had a single-platform release for *Hum Aapke Hain Koun..!* in Bombay. For other territories, they handpicked theatres for the film's release and the prints were given to the exhibitors only after the theatres had agreed to upgrade the sound as well as visual quality as required.

The upgradation resulted in a huge hike in ticket rates, phenomenal for way back in the 1990s. Surprisingly, the families that did not visit the sub-standard, run-down theatres, came back in full force to watch the film. The film smashed all box-office records by an enormous margin. The release size of the film kept expanding every month and it went on for a successful run for over 150 weeks. It also raked in over ₹70 crore at the box office then and broke the previous record of the highest-grossing Indian film, *Sholay*. Taking inflation into account, *Hum Aapke Hain Koun..!* remains the highest-grossing Bollywood film ever. It was estimated that only in Liberty Cinema, South Bombay, twenty lakh patrons thronged to watch the film.

The film won five Filmfare awards, at the 40th year of the awards, including Best Film, Best Director and Best Actress, in addition to the National Film Award for Best Popular Film Providing Wholesome Entertainment. A special screening of the film was held for the then President of India, Shankar Dayal Sharma, at the Rashtrapati Bhavan. Dubbed in Tamil as *Ambaalayam*, it had a successful run. In Telegu, it was titled *Premalayam* and ran over hundred days in fourteen centres. Internationally, *Hum Aapke Hain Koun..!* ran successfully for fifty weeks in London's Belle-Vue Cinema. The theatre was booked for only three weeks, as the property had to go for renovation. But the collection of the film was so tremendous that theatre owners decided to postpone the renovation. A musical production titled *14 songs, 2 weddings and a funeral,* designed on the film, played successfully in the theatres of London. In Canada, the film ran in Toronto's Albion Cinema for seventy-five weeks and was a runaway hit.

Madhuri was reportedly paid more than Salman for *Hum Aapke Hain Koun..!* But the box-office success of the film effortlessly slid Salman into the shoes of a superstar.

No hero, before Salman, had seen the mad hysteria that he was experiencing. Riding the wave of success, little did Salman know that come 1995, another Pathan would be sharing a part of the pie, and inscribing his name in the annals of history.

14

Shah Rukh Khan:
The Badshah of Bollywood

ithout knowing it, Yash Chopra touched Shah Rukh's life at the tender age of nine. Those were times when a school-going Shah Rukh used to fail miserably in Hindi. His mother had a unique way of inspiring her son. She told him that if he achieved a 10/10 in Hindi, she would take him to watch a Hindi movie in the theatre. This was a dream come true for Shah Rukh. Although Shah Rukh's family did not have the money to indulge in such luxuries then, his mother was certain this prize would spark her son's interest and motivate him to work on the subject.

Well, Shah Rukh got the 10/10. Later in life he confessed, 'I did copy the answer to one of the questions from my friend, Dhiraj Upadhay, who was very good in Hindi.' His mother kept her word and off they went to Vivek Cinema in Patel Nagar, Delhi. As soon as Shah Rukh stepped inside the theatre, his eyes brightened up. He was so short then, that he had to sit on his mother's handbag to view the screen. The world of fantasy that unfurled before him would leave a permanent mark on his young mind. The magic bug of the movies had stung Shah Rukh. He had fallen in love with the movies. The film was *Joshila*, directed by none other than Chopra himself.

Fast forwarding through life, Shah Rukh always looked up

to Chopra and held him in reverence. During the filming of *Darr*, Chopra was the esteemed captain of the ship while his sons, Aditya and Uday, were Shah Rukh's friends with whom he hung out. During this time, Aditya, who had been around his dad's sets since the age of four with a viewfinder hung around his neck, was planning to direct his own film, tentatively titled *Auzaar*. He shared this thought with Shah Rukh. With a name like *Auzaar*, Shah Rukh had assumed that this too would be a thriller. When Aditya narrated to him the story of Raj and Simran, where Raj was a yuppie hero romancing Simran and singing songs to her on scenic locations, Shah Rukh fell off the chair. It was a big 'no' from him.

Shah Rukh's Deewaar

Shah Rukh felt that Raj's character in the film was a pansy. His exact words were, 'It's the role of a wimp. I would feel like a wimp, a pansy.' Moreover, Shah Rukh was almost twenty-six when he entered the movie world and he definitely did not see himself running around trees and heroines. Aamir and Salman were already the romantic heartthrobs of the nation. Shah Rukh wanted to carve his own niche.

He had never forgotten the discouraging remark of his friend, a director, who had sat Shah Rukh down and said, 'You are very ugly. And being ugly necessarily means you do bad-guy roles. You aren't the romantic-hero type. Your face is not chocolatey enough.' Shah Rukh too believed that he could not fit into the shoes of a romantic hero.

Fortunately for him, the Chopras believed differently. Over weeks and several meetings, Aditya tried to convince Shah Rukh, but he was adamant. Aditya's spirit was dampened by an unenthusiastic Shah Rukh and he tried alternate options like Saif Ali Khan and some others, but his heart was set only on Shah Rukh. This choice was supported by his mother, Pamela, who believed that Shah Rukh had in him the charisma to be every woman's dream man and every mother's dream son.

Aditya was persistent and pursued Shah Rukh, until finally, along with Yash Chopra, they were able to convince him of the fact that Shah Rukh might be a star, but he would never become a superstar if he didn't do a romantic film. Shah Rukh finally agreed to play Raj only because of his faith in Yash and Aditya Chopra. Kajol, who was already a successful pair with Shah Rukh after *Baazigar*, was signed to play Simran, and the film, now titled *Dilwale Dulhania Le Jayenge*, rolled.

The unit travelled together in a bus to all the outdoor locales, stayed together and bonded like a big fat Indian family. Yash Chopra donned the role of the perfect producer and the magic genie for his son. He went out of his way to make available everything that the film needed at any time. Aditya was headlong into every detail, overworked and sleep-deprived. Aditya's assistant, Karan Johar, became friends with Shah Rukh, and the two would keep awake at nights, talking films. Kajol and Shah Rukh also strengthened their friendship further and were a riot together.

While the two were shooting a tricky romantic scene for the film in Switzerland, both actors slipped into fits of giggling. This was the scene where Simran (Kajol) gets drunk at night and wakes up the next morning to find herself in bed with Raj (Shah Rukh) and wearing his clothes. Every time Shah Rukh pulled down his jacket zipper to show Kajol lipstick marks, both of them would burst out laughing and neither could keep a straight face. After running through three magazines of expensive raw stock, director Aditya lost his patience and called for a break. Finally, after some firm counselling from the director, the cameras rolled again and this time, the two actors were at their professional best. They managed to contain their giggles until a relieved Aditya screamed 'Cut'.

Shah Rukh's gentlemanly nature and professional camaraderie made him the favourite with all his co-stars. Himani Shivpuri, who had made her big-screen debut with Salman in *Hum Aapke Hain Koun..!* played Kajol's bua (aunt) in *Dilwale Dulhania Le Jayenge*. She fondly remembers Shah Rukh's supportive gesture towards her during the iconic scene in which Raj helps her choose her outfit for the wedding. Though they did not have any combined shots together in the scene, Shah Rukh went out of his way to be present on the set and give all his cues himself. Usually when an actor is not being filmed, his lines that are cues to the other actor are spoken by the assistant director.

Hailing from a theatre background, Shah Rukh instinctively knew the importance of cues and that his participation would better the scene and his co-star's reaction would be more natural. 'Shah Rukh was a bounty of ceaseless energy,' recalls co-star Farida Jalal, who played Kajol's mother in the film. 'He never ever tired of repeated rehearsals or from giving every bit of his contribution to make the film a little bit better than it already was. Working with Shah Rukh was a treat and he even made adversity at the shoot feel easy with his helpful nature.'

One such adversity was the difficult situation during the filming of the song 'Tujhe dekha toh yeh jaana sanam' in Haryana. The film ran into a tight spot with permissions and the locals. The unit is said to have attained permission from the panchayat to shoot for the song on a small plot of land with bright-yellow mustard flowers. But the local residents objected vehemently. That's when Shah Rukh intervened and patiently spoke in his Haryanvi accent, leaving the locals mesmerized. Gradually, the residents calmed down and the unit started setting up for the shot.

Troubles, especially with the shooting of the songs, were a bit of an event during the shoot of *Dilwale Dulhania Le Jayenge*. At an outdoor schedule, choreographer Saroj Khan could not reach on time. The unit was waiting and time was running out. Shah Rukh stepped in to help again. He called his choreographer friend, Farah Khan, in London at 6 a.m., to join their sets. But Farah was committed to another film, so she could not make it. Aditya refused to stop work and decided to film the song himself. Whilst he had just started the sequence with Shah Rukh and Kajol on a bridge, Saroj showed up. She apologized and the shoot started. But Aditya resolved that he would never work with her again. Farah joined the *Dilwale Dulhania Le Jayenge* unit for the remaining song, 'Ruk ja o dil diwane', and the picturization of that song had its own unique story.

Shah Rukh, at that time, was also shooting for Subhash Ghai's *Trimurti*. Date problems led to Shah Rukh shooting in double shifts. From 11 a.m. to 3 p.m., he would shoot for *Dilwale Dulhania Le Jayenge*, and then from 3 p.m. to 10 p.m., he would move on to *Trimurti*. The unit had only four days to shoot the 'Ruk ja' song. Aditya was unhappy, but Farah rose to the occasion and was quick to improvise. She drew inspiration from dancing king, Shammi Kapoor, fused them with groovy twists and long shots that would take less time to shoot. Thus the dance steps with the table cloth were done in one take and Shah Rukh got it right the very first time. The song would not have made it through its tight deadline without the prompt and perfect timing of King Khan to learn his steps and perform it with ease.

Shah Rukh fondly remembers some contributions that went on to make the song special. One was how Karan Johar, then an assistant in the direction department, and who also played the role of his friend in the film, doubled as an opera singer in the song. Another decision taken on set during the making of the song was that Shah Rukh, who was carrying Kajol, would drop her, much to her surprise. Shah Rukh and Farah wanted a spontaneous reaction from Kajol and that's what they got. The song went on to become a memorable part of the film.

After *Baazigar* and *Darr*, Shah Rukh came to believe that including a little bloodshed was his lucky charm for a hit film. He was keen to have a dash of action in the otherwise romantic family drama. Hence in the pre-climax action scene, he fights Kuljeet Singh (played by Parmeet Sethi) and his friends at the railway station.

Before signing the film, Shah Rukh felt he was anything but the character of Raj. But over the course of filming *Dilwale Dulhania Le Jayenge,* he changed his mind. 'I think 90 per cent of the character of Raj is like me. So yeah, if girls think they can't find Raj, they can always call me,' he joked much later. As a matter of fact, in an interview with *Filmfare* in April 1996, Shah Rukh remarked that his marriage was 'straight out of *Dilwale Dulhania Le Jayenge.* His wife Gauri's parents were dead set against the marriage'. But he managed to convince all her relatives one by one, just like Raj did.

After watching the film in a trial show, Shah Rukh told Yash Chopra that *Dilwale Dulhania Le Jayenge* to him was what *Deewaar* was to Amitabh Bachchan—the one film that was going to make his career. However, Aditya was worried about the climax. Shah Rukh's emotional speech in the twentieth reel—where he leaves his lady-love Simran (Kajol) with her father (Amrish Puri) and departs from the house, telling her that he would not run away with her unless her father gave his consent to their relationship—was the scene that would either make or break the film.

On the day of the release, Aditya did not go to see the audience's reaction in the first half of the film. Along with one of his assistants, he reached Gaiety Theatre in Bandra just after the interval. Soon, Shah Rukh's speech began. Aditya crossed his fingers and put his head into his knees. There was complete silence in the theatre.

During that time, Shah Rukh was shooting in Jaipur for a film called *Chaahat* with Mahesh Bhatt. He was nervous too. Moreover, the producer of *Baazigar*, Ratan Jain, had predicted to Shah Rukh after seeing the trial of *Dilwale Dulhania Le Jayenge* that, 'Don't mind, but this film will never work. People will not accept you as a romantic hero.'

Shah Rukh, with fingers crossed, visited a local theatre along with Bhatt and his leading lady in *Chaahat*, Pooja Bhatt. By the climax, the audience were mumbling and Shah Rukh panicked. But as it grew louder, he could hear the audience more clearly—they were repeating his lines with him. *Dilwale Dulhania Le Jayenge* had made it safely home and had begun climbing the ladder to blockbuster status.

Heir Apparent

On the first day of *Dilwale Dulhania Le Jayenge*'s release, in San Francisco's Naz Theatre, 1,000 people showed up to fill 720 seats. In those days, without online booking, people had to go to the theatre to buy their tickets. Not willing to disappoint so many people, the theatre proprietor, Shiraz Jiwani, had no choice but to run a second show at 1 a.m. and 680 people stayed on for it. More than 11,000 people saw the film in the first week alone. For three weeks, the theatre ran shows round the clock, starting the first one at 5 a.m. This unattractive timing, at the crack of dawn, did not dither the viewers. Jiwani eventually collected approximately $200,000 from the film.

In the United Kingdom, *Dilwale Dulhania Le Jayenge* ran for over a year, collecting £2.5 million.[36] The tickets were a steep £10 each, but the theatres were packed. Repeat runs of the film attracted a fair share of viewers.

Dilwale Dulhania Le Jayenge didn't match up to Salman's *Hum Aapke Hain Koun..!*'s collections, but it did make it to the list of ten most successful Hindi films ever.

In February 1996, at the 41st Filmfare Awards, *Dilwale Dulhania Le Jayenge* swept most categories. It bagged a total of eleven awards, including Best Director, Best Film, Best Actor in a lead role and Best Actress in a lead role, among others. A few months later, it won the National Film Award for Best Popular Film Providing Wholesome Entertainment. Aditya requested his father, Yash Chopra, to collect this prestigious recognition on his behalf.

After the film's success, the press positioned Shah Rukh Khan as the 'hottest star' of Bollywood. The December 1994 edition of *Movie* magazine had Shah Rukh's picture on the cover next to that of Amitabh Bachchan's. The headline read,

[36]Anupama Chopra, *Dilwale Dulhania Le Jayenge: A Modern Classic*, HarperCollins Publishers, India, 2016

'Heir Apparent?'

Dilwale Dulhania Le Jayenge indeed became Shah Rukh's *Deewaar*. Just like the 1975 blockbuster *Deewaar*, directed by Yash Chopra, created a brand of the Angry Young Man and sealed the position for Amitabh Bachchan as the iconic superstar in Bollywood, *Dilwale Dulhania Le Jayenge* created the brand of the coveted lover boy for Shah Rukh, which would last through generations. Yash Chopra went on to direct Shah Rukh's next smash hit, *Dil to Pagal Hai* and Shah Rukh as Rahul had now become the poster boy of romance.

Soon, Karan Johar, Aditya's assistant who played the cameo in *Dilwale Dulhania Le Jayenge*, came up with another love story, *Kuch Kuch Hota Hai*. The film celebrated traditional modernity in a spectacularly suave fashion. It gave the world of romance a Rahul who did not shy away from showing his tender side—as put in Shah Rukh's own words, 'A Pathan who can cry'. *Kuch Kuch Hota Hai* etched in stone the superstardom of Shah Rukh Khan.

The idea of *Kuch Kuch Hota Hai* had germinated during the filming of *Dilwale Dulhania Le Jayenge*, which was Karan Johar's training ground as a film-maker. He remembers vividly that it was during the shooting of the antara, or the second paragraph, of the iconic song 'Tujhe dekha toh yeh jaana sanam' that his world changed forever. It was very cold, so the unit had packed up for the day. While they were relaxing, Shah Rukh dropped a surprise on Johar. With a calm demeanour, he told Johar, 'You should become a director'. Johar *did* harbour dreams of becoming a director but had wanted to give himself preparation time of at least six or seven years before embarking on the journey of his independent project. Shah Rukh's proposal took him by complete surprise. Shah

Rukh told Johar that if he was ready to do the film right after *Dilwale Dulhania Le Jayenge*, then Shah Rukh would be a part of it. A film with Shah Rukh was a dream come true for Johar, but the idea of starting so soon had stumped him. Before he could recover from this jolt, in came his other friend, Kajol, and dropped another bomb. When Shah Rukh told her of his plans to star in Johar's film, she immediately said, 'I will also do it.' Johar suddenly had a cast on his hand but with very little time to prepare.

A dream star cast and the ideal break as a debuting director were on the plate for Johar, except for the fact that the story he had written needed another superstar to be cast in the supporting role. Nearly the entire industry had turned Johar down for this role. Then he met Salman at Chunky Pandey's party.

Salman asked him, 'I heard you have a role and no one is doing it.'

Johar mumbled, 'Yes.'

Salman: 'I will do it.'

Johar: 'Why are you doing this?'

Salman: 'I like your father.'

That's how Salman came on board. At that time, he was doing *Hum Dil De Chuke Sanam* and *Chori Chori Chupke Chupke*. Having to allot dates for so many commitments, Salman could only spare a couple of hours to shoot for *Kuch Kuch Hota Hai*. Farah Khan shot his introduction song with a lot of back shots, which were done by Farah's dancer, Richie, who luckily looked like Salman's body double.

Kuch Kuch Hota Hai too dominated the 44th Filmfare Awards in 1999, including a sweep of the major acting categories. Of the seventeen nominations that the film received, it won eight, with Shah Rukh ruling the stage and bagging the Best Actor once again. Incidentally, Salman too won the Best Supporting Actor for this film—nine years after his Best Male Debut award for *Maine Pyar Kiya*.

Both *Dilwale Dulhania Le Jayenge* and *Dil to Pagal Hai* from the house of Yash Raj Films and *Kuch Kuch Hota Hai* from Dharma Productions spun a magic world where Shah Rukh was the youth icon. For the first time, non-resident Indians (NRIs) thronged the theatres to watch Hindi films, and returns from overseas territories hit the roof. The three films went on to become all-time blockbusters with whopping collections of $4,800,000, $3,300,000 and $6,300,000 respectively just from overseas, which when added to the Indian gross collection summed up to over triple-figure crore worldwide collections.

Twenty years after the release of *Dilwale Dulhania Le Jayenge*, on the last day of United States' President Barack Obama's visit to India, he packed in a filmy punch when he addressed the crowd in Delhi's Siri Fort Auditorium in January 2015. Speaking to the gathering, he struck a chord with the youth, when he delivered the iconic dialogue from *Dilwale Dulhania Le Jayenge*, saying, '*Senorita, bade bade desho mein...* You know what I mean.' And that evoked a thunderous applause from university students and activists who comprised the gathering. *Dilwale Dulhania Le Jayenge* had successfully filtered through two decades—running successfully in Mumbai's Maratha Mandir Theatre for over 1,000 uninterrupted weeks—and remained relevant.

Even today, a poster of *Dilwale Dulhania Le Jayenge* hangs in Aditya's office where Shah Rukh had written:

Dear Adi, More than half my career ago, you gave me

a dream to cherish all my life. My kids will see it, my grandchildren will love it and I'm sure even in heaven they are playing our film—so my parents would have seen it too. Thanks for taking me to them and making me the star I'm today.

Once upon a time, 1950's Bollywood was ruled by Raj Kapoor, Dilip Kumar and Dev Anand—the triumvirate of Hindi Cinema. Raj Kapoor had modelled himself on Charlie Chaplin's image of a 'tramp'. Dilip Kumar had defined himself with meticulous method acting. Dev Anand had stolen the hearts of many a woman with his Gregory Peck-inspired stylish persona. This quintessential trinity of the 1950s is remembered by their iconic hits; their styles continue to woo the common man even today.

History repeated itself in the late 1990s and a new triumvirate had arrived—Aamir, Salman and Shah Rukh. They had become an indisputable troika.

Well, almost. Except that a young boy was preparing day in, day out to challenge the trio's invincibility. The question was, could he?

Sanjukta Nandy

15

Karan, Arjun and the Tsunami

Two young girls were speeding in a car through the by-lanes of Juhu when they spotted a handsome, twenty-six-year-old young man, with green eyes and a rugged look, chatting with a friend outside his house. The car passed them, went a few feet ahead before screeching to a halt. Then it reversed and one of the girls screamed, 'Oh my god! Is that Hrithik?' The young man smiled and waved back. The girl at the wheel shrieked and pressed on the accelerator, instead of the brake, thus ramming the car into a tree. Luckily, this incident did not have a casualty but the same could not be said about the nation then. There was something about this boy that had cast a magic spell on the audience and had sent perfectly sane people into a maniacal craze, driving them towards insanity. This story, which is more fact than fiction, was actually accounted by a journalist in an article in March 2000.[37]

Come the new millennium, no one could have predicted that a homegrown Greek God would rock the nation. The media widely speculated that his overnight stardom had rocked

---

[37]Madhu Jain, 'In a Bollywood dominated by the Khans, Hrithik Roshan suddenly becomes a national craze', Indiatoday.in, 20 March 2000, accessed 3 October 2019, https://www.indiatoday.in/magazine/cover-story/story/20000320-in-a-bollywood-dominated-by-the-khans-hrithik-roshan-suddenly-becomes-a-national-craze-777238-2000-03-20

the foundation of the well-rooted Khan-dom too. Ironically, the same Khans, particularly Shah Rukh and Salman, played a role in Hrithik's grooming to stardom.

Hrithik's journey in films started as an assistant director to his father, director and producer, Rakesh Roshan. Shah Rukh-starrers *King Uncle* and *Koyla*, besides the Shah Rukh-Salman money-spinner, *Karan Arjun*, served as his training grounds. The Khans too grew fond of this lanky, shy, intelligent boy.

After the mega success of *Karan Arjun*, which then grossed over ₹43 crore worldwide, Roshan signed Shah Rukh for his next film, *Koyla*. Hrithik had now decided to pursue acting. He again joined as an assistant director to Rakesh Roshan in *Koyla*. Hrithik closely watched Shah Rukh emote and perform the role of Shankar. It was a difficult part, as Shah Rukh had to play the role of a mute and loyal slave. He had to depict intense emotions, but without words. Hrithik not only watched Shah Rukh perform, but also enacted Shah Rukh's scenes from *Koyla*, when back home. Then, he would film himself to find out if he was doing it right. After training as an actor at Kishore Namit Kapoor's acting school and Anupam Kher's academy, besides having worked with Hindi and Urdu elocution teachers, Hrithik felt confident enough to face the camera. He also approached Salman to help him build his body.

Shaping up with Salman as his mentor was a huge step forward for Hrithik. Protein shakes, low-fat diet and pumping iron resulted in chiselled biceps. When Salman realized that the young Hrithik was quick to pick up instructions, he prophesized, '*Tu star hai, tu pakka star banega* (You are star material. You will be a star without a doubt).'

Meanwhile, Rakesh Roshan was planning his next film after *Koyla*. His first choice was Shah Rukh but when it did not work out, he went out and made the film with Hrithik in it.

That's Star Power

January 2000. As the new millennium came in with a bang, so did *Kaho Naa... Pyaar Hai*, which marked Hrithik's debut as an actor. He played a double role in this film. Two and a half hours of the film and Hrithik's life and the scape of Bollywood changed forever.

Anxious in anticipation, on the day of the release, Hrithik, along with friend Kunal Kapoor, went to one of Mumbai's suburban, single-screen theatres to gauge the response to his film. Kunal remembers what happened during the interval:

> I saw the public pouncing on Hrithik. Some were pulling at his shirt, others were reaching for his hair, while many tried to hug him. He was being mobbed. I somehow reached him and steered him out of there. He was completely shocked. He just looked at me and said, 'Is this good or bad?' I said this is great!

Before the release of *Kaho Naa... Pyaar Hai*, Hrithik was invited to an event by the newspaper, *Dainik Jagran*. When Hrithik was at the airport, it was his father who was recognized and hounded by the crowd. Following the release of the film, when Hrithik and his father were spotted at the Lucknow airport, it was a different scenario, recalls eyewitness, journalist and film critic, Ajay Brahmatmaj. As soon as the crowd saw Hrithik, there was a murmur that rose amongst them. Before anyone could react, Hrithik was encircled by fans who could not believe their luck at having spotted their new-found matinee sizzler. They pounced on Hrithik in wild hysteria. So intense was the admiration and pandemonium that finally the police had to be called in to manage the star-struck crowd and the star, baffled by his new-found stardom, was whisked away to safety.

Even weeks after the film's release, the advance-booking queues continued to snake outside theatres. Tickets sold at ₹500 in the black market. The first week obtained 99.87 per cent returns from ticket sales. The second week kept up the tempo at 99.69 per cent and even the third didn't slacken at 99.18 per cent in Mumbai. These numbers, calculated as a percentage from territories all over India where Mumbai is the largest territory, were at par with Shah Rukh's *Kuch Kuch Hota Hai*. The film industry was sitting up to watch the new arrival.

Hrithik's posters were selling off the shelves and there was demand for more before the stock could be replenished. Sriniwas Sadani, proprietor of Hallmark store in Kolkata's Elgin Road, was taken aback by this frenzied demand. 'No one—no cricketer, film star or pop musician—has sold so many posters,' he said. 'People have forgotten Shah Rukh Khan,' he added. There were new diehard fans. Actor Govinda's daughter insisted on Hrithik cutting her birthday cake, to which Govinda had commented, 'Now I know what a star is.' Eleven-year-old Maia Sethna, the little scene-stealer in Deepa Mehta's film *Earth*, said, 'Hrithik's cool, I really like him. I used to like Shah Rukh Khan.'

At the 46th Filmfare Awards in February 2001, Hrithik won the Best Actor as well as the Best Male Debut trophies. Shah Rukh had to be content with the Best Actor in the Critic's Choice category for *Mohabbatein*. In November 2001, Hrithik shared *Filmfare*'s cover space with Shah Rukh and Amitabh, titled 'That's Star Power'.

Hrithik's success became more obvious during the days when the political scenario in India was dominated by the Atal Bihari Vajpayee government. This was the time, as analysed by Ajay Brahmatmaj, when the socio-psychology of the country was veering towards saffron endorsement. The mood of film media writing was coloured saffron too. Scanning the scenario then, he states, that it was a time when the Khans were in their thirties. They were well embossed into the map of Hindi cinema for almost a decade. The arrival of this young, Hindu star with a frenzied fan following was further sensationalized in the media by adding a colour/angle of religion to it. The newspaper and magazines were quick with their stories of the Khan-dom being challenged and the young Roshan replacing the trio. Shah Rukh's *Phir Bhi Dil Hai Hindustani* released on 21 January 2000 failed, while Hrithik's *Kaho Naa... Pyaar Hai* released on 14 January 2000 went on to become a blockbuster. People in the industry speculated about writing Shah Rukh off. He was also accused of being insecure and mocking Hrithik in a Pepsi commercial directed by ace ad man, Prahlad Kakkar. Kakkar, however, took Shah Rukh's side and called this criticism unjustified. He further clarified that the humour added with the Hrithik lookalike in the ad was not Shah Rukh's idea but his own. The media, however, kept on digging and interpreting more instances that corroborated this competition. During an award show then, while Hrithik was on an award sweeping spree, the camera constantly panned to Shah Rukh seated in the audience. Many articles on how devastated the Khan was with the advent of this new star were written in film and news columns.

Start of a Cold War

Meanwhile, Shah Rukh's favourite director, Karan Johar, had signed Hrithik for a film even before the release of *Kaho Naa... Pyaar Hai*. Johar had met him at a Manish Malhotra store with his mother. Once Johar saw the rough cut of the film, he knew that his prediction was right about Hrithik. In Johar's film, *Kabhi Khushi Kabhie Gham...*, Hrithik shared screen time with Shah Rukh and Amitabh. The film went on to become a hugely successful film, with a worldwide gross collection then of over ₹130 crore and received fifteen nominations at the 47th Filmfare Awards held in February 2002. Shah Rukh was nominated for Best Actor and Hrithik for Best Supporting Actor. However, it was Aamir who won the Best Actor that year for his film *Lagaan*.

Soon after, a buzz of a cold war between Shah Rukh and Hrithik gained momentum. It was heard that Shah Rukh's wife, Gauri and Hrithik's wife, Sussanne had gone on to become good friends. Shah Rukh and Hrithik were initially formal and awkward when they met each other with their spouses but eventually warmed up to each other. When Hrithik did not receive the national award for *Lakshya*, it was Shah Rukh who called him and said that for him, Hrithik was a winner. This warm overture meant a lot to Hrithik. It was widely spoken that Gauri, who had by then acquired maturity and experience in having to share her star-husband with his fans, did pass on tips to Sussanne about the same. The two star wives even appeared together in the first season of *Koffee with Karan* where they were naughty enough to call up their respective husbands and find out the answers to Johar's questions on how well they knew their spouses. While the girls had fun on the show, their respective husbands too joined in and the cold vibes ebbed away. Over time, Shah Rukh and Hrithik warmed up to each other. They walked the ramp together, along with Amitabh Bachchan. Shah Rukh also attended Hrithik's birthday bash and danced through the night.

Much later, in January 2017, the box office saw the clash of two big releases, Shah Rukh's *Raees* and Hrithik's *Kaabil*. Rakesh Roshan had stated, 'I had announced the date for *Kaabil* earlier. If they are coming on the same date, then I can't do anything about it.' Senior Roshan added, 'I don't know what they will eventually decide. We're here to make films, not create controversies. As far as Shah Rukh is concerned, he's like a younger brother to me. I gave him a break in *King Uncle*, and then worked with him in *Karan Arjun* and *Koyla*.' Roshan also mentioned that if he ever did a two-hero film like *Karan Arjun*, he would now cast Hrithik and Shah Rukh in it.

Industry reports suggested that before the release of the two films, Shah Rukh had been in talks with Hrithik and his father, along with the producers of *Raees*, Farhan Akhtar and Ritesh Sidhwani. Both the parties tried to work out a way in which the box-office clash could be avoided. However, the films did clash on the Republic Day of 2017. *Raees* had an excellent opening but went on to get a tag of a semi hit. *Kaabil* too got a lukewarm response from the audience. It is rumoured even now, that the once affable relationship of the Khan and the Roshans still bears signs of this strain.

Even the affable relationship between Hrithik and Salman changed over time. Hrithik had once revealed that during the preview of his debut film when all the seats were full, Salman had stood for three hours, with his hand on Hrithik's shoulder, watching the film. Such was their camaraderie. Hrithik by his own admission at the Filmfare Awards had thanked Salman for mentoring him while lifting the trophy for *Kaho Naa... Pyaar Hai*. Salman in appreciation of the young boy's success had gifted him an expensive watch. But years down the line, post the release of Sanjay Leela Bhansali's Hrithik-starrer *Guzaarish*, Salman was reported to have said, '*Arre, usme toh makkhi udd rahi thi, lekin koi machhar bhi nahi gaya dekhne. Arre, koi kutta bhi nahin gaya* (There was a fly buzzing in the film but not even a mosquito went to see the film. Not even a dog went).'[38]

'I've always known Salman to be a good man, someone I've looked up to, admired and still do. He's always been a hero and always will be. But yes, it's not heroic to laugh or make fun of a filmmaker just because his box office collections are not up there with yours,' shared Hrithik in a reply to *The Times of India*.[39]

The dent in Salman and Hrithik's relationship carried on for a while, but all was well when in May 2013, the Roshan boy visited Salman's store, Being Human, and shopped for his clothes. The highly emotional Salman was happy to know that Hrithik believed in his Being Human endeavour. The white flag flapped strong and motioned in the winds of peace over time. Soon, Hrithik shook a leg with Salman at the grand

[38]*India Today* Web Desk, 'When "ungraceful" Salman Khan said Hrithik Roshan's *Guzaarish* was "not seen by even a dog"', *India Today*, 17 May 2018, accessed 16 July 2019, https://www.indiatoday.in/movies/celebrities/story/when-ungraceful-salman-khan-said-hrithik-roshan-s-guzaarish-was-not-seen-by-even-a-dog-1235377-2018-05-17

[39]Kunal M. Shah and Subhash K. Jha, 'Salman should show some grace: Hrithik', *The Times of India*, 3 December 2010, accessed 16 September 2019, https://timesofindia.indiatimes.com/entertainment/hindi/bollywood/news/Salman-should-show-some-grace-Hrithik/articleshow/7033773.cms

finale of *Bigg Boss* Season 10 in January 2017 and after the show he took to social media and posted: '*Kaun Shahenshah, kaun Sultan*. At the end of it, we are all brothers.'

Nothing lasts forever in the film industry. It's a game that changes every Friday. A world of drama that has tremendous amount of elasticity to encapsulate all the stars, on a pedestal, whoever manages to ring in the pennies at the box office. A world that catapults an actor to dizzy heights and at times, plunges him to rock bottom depending on his performance on a particular weekend.

The Khans *did* survive the tsunami of this mega wave. But this did not guarantee that there would not be a dearth of howling rough winds rocking their boats in the near future.

16

The Break-up:
Yeh Bandhan Toh... [40]

'Shah Rukh and I will never patch up.'

So said Salman in an interview to a tabloid in 2008.[41]

'I am not going to deny that there are issues between us. I am a primitive man, born in today's time. I can't fake anything. If there is a problem, I am not going to deny it. We have had problems before, but this time, I don't think we can sort them out. We cannot be friends again. I think it is better to declare that, rather than put on a fake facade of being friends, back-biting each other,' added the outspoken Khan.

Nearly eight years had passed. It was an early morning in July 2016, at Bandstand, Bandra. A regular day at the promenade with both young and old engrossed in their exercise routines. Two men cycled down the promenade. This would have otherwise been an ordinary sight but seeing the two men, each and every head turned as they stopped to stare.

One of them was dressed in the previous night's crisp formals, now slightly wrinkled, while the other was in his

---

[40]Shah Rukh and Salman's brotherhood anthem from *Karan Arjun*
[41]Rediff, 'Salman: Shah Rukh and I can't be friends', rediff.com, 11 August 2008, accessed 3 October 2019, https://m.rediff.com/movies/2008/aug/11salman.htm

casual T-shirt and trousers. The two cyclists were followed by an entourage of bodyguards, staff and their BMWs. They seemed to be best friends.

As they came closer to the crowd, there were gasps and murmurs. People went into a frenzy taking pictures with their mobile phones. It is not every day that one saw the 'Karan Arjun' of Bollywood, cycling together on the streets of Bandra, soaking in the fresh morning breeze and enjoying the glow of the rising sun. It did not take much time for Shah Rukh and Salman's brotherhood-endorsement picture to go viral on the Internet.

All of this started with Shah Rukh's impromptu decision the previous night. It had been just another rainy evening when Shah Rukh had wrapped up a brand event and decided not to go back home. He wanted to catch up with an old friend. He called Salman and dropped in at his house. They chatted over biryani, kebabs and the best delicacies at Khan's home. Post dinner, the duo stayed awake all night, chatting into the wee hours of the morning. Then Salman made an impromptu suggestion to take a bicycle ride. Shah Rukh, despite being in formals from the previous night's event, was gung-ho about it. He called his son, Aryan, to join them. Aryan cycled from his house, Mannat, to Salman's Galaxy Apartments, which is barely a kilometre away. Salman got his security to bring out his two favourite two-wheelers. The men, along with Aryan in tow, hit the streets at about 5:45 a.m. They were back as friends.

Their friendship dated back to the times when Shah Rukh was just an entrant into the film industry. They had first met at a Bandra gym. Shah Rukh could not help but admire Salman's sculpted body and his dedication towards working out. He once said, 'When I had come to Mumbai, Salman and his entire family welcomed me with open arms. Not only me, but they warmly welcomed Gauri too. It felt we were amongst friends and family. I respect him a lot. I have always told my children that if there was one family that looked after our family, that was Salman's.' Shah Rukh has also gone on to say that if he was not in town and his kids or family ever needed help, they would reach out to Salman and he was certain that Salman and his family would be there for them.

Years ago, in 1993, when Shah Rukh was returning from Mehboob Studio, after the shooting of *King Uncle*, and was walking back to his house—he used to then live at director Aziz Mirza's house—he met Salim Khan on the road. Salim saab said, '*Janab aap toh star ban gaye*! (You have become a star).' Salim saab then mentioned that he was on his way back from a hair-cutting salon, where he had been asked if he wanted a Shah Rukh Khan haircut. He added that when a salon endorses an actor's hairstyle, it can safely be said that the actor has been promoted to star status. Shah Rukh remembers this as one of his earliest memories of fond interactions with Salman's family.

Shah Rukh remembers an incident from the premier of *Dilwale Dulhania Le Jayenge*. He had a couple of friends sitting beside him at the screening. There was a scene in the film where Shah Rukh says, '*Raj, agar yeh tujhe pyaar karti hai, toh palat ke dekhegi. Palat. Palat. Palat* (Raj, if she loves you, she will turn around).' At that point, one of his friends told him, 'It seems like you'll kill her, like you killed the girl in *Baazigar*. If you weren't in this movie, it would do really well.' Shah Rukh was crestfallen. But the first person, apart from the unit, who patted Shah Rukh on the back and gave him a positive review, was none other than Salman, who assured him that it was a 'great film'. And this not only encouraged him immensely but stayed back in Shah Rukh's mind.

In their early days, Salman and Shah Rukh would meet on special occasions and parties. But gradually, their acquaintance grew into friendship that further developed into brotherhood when they signed *Karan Arjun*. Salman later said, 'It was a story of brothers from not one but two lifetimes. So, if we were not like brothers in real life, we would never be able to pull it off on screen.'

Karan Arjun marked the beginning of a stronger bond between the two mega stars. Originally titled *Kaynath*, Shah Rukh and Salman were not the first choices of director Rakesh Roshan. He originally wanted Ajay Devgn and Sunny Deol. Akshay Kumar, too, was considered for the role of Karan. Unfortunately, this project did not take off as planned. Roshan was not able to put together a cast that he felt could justify his story. Then Shah Rukh, who had worked with Roshan in *King Uncle,* was approached. He was prompt to come on board and also recommended Salman to Roshan for the other role. Salman agreed immediately and the film went on the floors.

While Salman was an easy-going actor, Shah Rukh was committed and passionate about his craft. They made the perfect combination for a hit pair. Salman later confessed that whenever he watched *Karan Arjun*, he would get moist-eyed, as happy memories of the filming came flooding back to his mind.

During the shoot, which was in Chomu, near Jaipur, the duo had the option of staying in the luxurious Samode Palace, Jaipur. But they decided to opt for a smaller space with only fifteen rooms. The rooms were small and the beds even smaller. But the space had a warm, homely charm to it. Salman's brother, Sohail, often visited and then all three would share a room together. Shah Rukh would often snore loudly and the brothers would push him off the bed to wake him up.

The two were known for their no-nonsense approach too. The film had a very rude production controller who had ticked off nearly everyone in the unit with his foul language and temper. He would even behave rudely with the leads, including Shah Rukh, who was known for his grace and good manners. Salman hatched a plan to set the chap right.

It was a chilly night. The staff was put up in tents near the hotel, as there were not enough rooms for the entire unit. Salman sneaked into the production controller's tent and let out a pipe of chilling cold water into his tent. When the man came back to his tent, he found it flooded with cold water. His bedding and belongings were all dripping wet. The man was furious and yelled all night. Eventually, the message reached him loud and clear and he never ever misbehaved.

The two friends had even put up a small gym near the accommodation. They would work out and party together during the making of the film. Co-star Aasif Sheikh remembers that his room was just next to the gym and he would hear the duo chat while they kept up their exercise regime even late into the night. Shah Rukh had never worked out before, while Salman was an expert. He encouraged Shah Rukh to start working out, something his *Om Shanti Om* six-pack abs would raise a toast to. A tank in the premise was converted into a swimming pool and the Khans would often be swimming when they were not shooting. The small space and the group activities facilitated the bonding and today, Salman adds with a glint of humour, 'We saved Rakesh Roshan a lot of money.'

Rakesh Roshan made even more money when the film became a mammoth success. The Khans became synonymous with their characters and from then on, they were often referred to as Karan and Arjun.

The special bond of friendship between them grew deeper with time over various occasions and events. In 1998, Shah Rukh won the Best Actor for *Dil to Pagal Hai* at the Zee Cine Awards. He came on stage and said, 'There's a very close friend of mine who has been saying, "Shah Rukh, *tereko humesha award milta hai, mereko nahi milta hai* (Shah Rukh, you always get awards and I don't)".' He then invited 'the friend', Salman, on stage to deliver the thank you speech on his behalf. Salman came on stage and hugged Shah Rukh warmly. Quickly, he donned on his funny self and went on to fake a few tears. Enacting in a voice choked with emotion and holding the trophy, he said, 'Oh my god, I can't believe this.'

Salman readily agreed to act with Shah Rukh in *Kuch Kuch Hota Hai* when nearly the entire industry was insecure to act in a film where Shah Rukh dominated screen time. On receiving the Filmfare Best Actor for the film, Shah Rukh had said, 'Salman is the only man whose body is matched by my luscious lips.' Salman won the Best Supporting Actor for his role in the film, and said, 'Now I hope Shah Rukh supports me for the rest of my life.'

In 2000, Shah Rukh made a guest appearance in the Salman-starrer, *Har Dil Jo Pyaar Karega...* and they worked together in *Hum Tumhare Hain Sanam*. But little did they know that the first cracks in their friendship would arise the same year.

Of Brawls and Brotherhood

It was on the sets of Shah Rukh's home production, *Chalte Chalte*, which starred Salman's then-girlfriend Aishwarya Rai, did matters turn sour. Salman stormed onto the sets one day and disrupted the shooting. It was reported that the two lovers allegedly came to a fist fight. Subsequently, Aishwarya lost the film and a cold war started to brew between the two Khans. But, in 2004, they buried the hatchet at Farah Khan's sangeet (pre-wedding celebrations) in Mumbai. Choreographer Farah Khan was a close friend of both Salman and Shah Rukh since their early days in the industry. Her wedding celebrations brought the Khans face to face on the same platform where they again warmed up to each other. The two of them let their guard down and were back in their camaraderie mode, dancing and celebrating together through the night.

Shah Rukh had asked Salman to make a guest appearance in *Om Shanti Om* and Salman promptly agreed. Later, Salman reportedly asked Shah Rukh to do a role in *Main Aurr Mrs Khanna* in 2008, but Shah Rukh declined the request, allegedly citing date issues. It is believed that this triggered a discontent in Salman and a simmering resentment brewed in Salman's heart since then. It was the setting for a terrible fight.

On 16 July 2008, Salman hosted a star-studded birthday bash for Katrina Kaif at the Olive Bar & Kitchen in Mumbai. It was attended by numerous celebrities. Salman is believed to have been drinking since early evening. He was in a foul mood, even before Shah Rukh and Gauri came in.

On seeing Shah Rukh, Salman took constant digs to instigate him. He reportedly compared their reality quiz shows, *10 Ka Dum* and *Kya Aap Paanchvi Pass Se Tez Hain?* Salman claimed that his show *10 Ka Dum* had garnered more TRPs than Shah Rukh's show. Some even believe that Salman's digs at Shah Rukh were sharp and stinging, insinuating that the latter's show was a dud and the host was nothing but a 'Paanchvi

Class Mein Fail'. Shah Rukh initially did not get provoked, but finally hit back, remarking about Salman's ex-lady-love, Aishwarya Rai. This took an ugly turn and led to a physical fight between the two of them. Ultimately, Gauri separated the two and was able to drag Shah Rukh away from the brawl. The never-before-prophesized crack was now wide open for all to see. Aamir, who was also present at the party, tried his best to resolve the dispute. But the two Khans were not in a mood for a compromise. Both were supported by their respective well-wishers. The industry was split into two distinct camps following this falling-out.

Later, in 2008, in an interview, Shah Rukh said that Salman was angry because he had turned down a film.[42] Salman retorted through the press saying that he had never offered him the film in the first place. He also said, 'Shah Rukh was like my brother. He used to call me "sir, sir" during his struggling days. I have seen him go from door to door asking for work. He has become a different person now.'

In 2010, Salman reportedly said, 'Only God can come and make us friends again. And that is not happening.' In 2011, on Karan Johar's chat show, *Koffee with Karan*, Shah Rukh said, 'If Salman is angry with me, it's 100 per cent my fault.' Salman responded stating that Shah Rukh's public apology to him was only to bring in higher TRPs. He brushed off the gesture and retorted that they lived within a stone's throw and if Shah Rukh really meant it, he would have just come home and spoken to him.

---

[42]*India Today* Web Desk, 'When SRK said it is 100 per cent his fault if Salman is angry with him', *India Today*, August 2018, accessed 3 October 2019, https://www.indiatoday.in/movies/celebrities/story/when-srk-said-it-is-100-per-cent-his-fault-if-salman-is-angry-with-him-1308659-2018-08-08

Bitterness sizzled between Salman and Shah Rukh. Aamir, the other Khan of the trio, is believed to have stood by his friendship with Salman and had tried to patch things up between the warring friends. However, neither side budged nor did the two families ever make any public statement. And one day in 2011, following the release of the Salman-starrer *Bodyguard*, and after the release of *Ra.One*, a Blackberry status of Salman's sister, Alvira, surfaced. It said: 'Even a superhero needs a Bodyguard!' At that time, Salman's *Bodyguard* turned out to be commercially successful, while Shah Rukh's *Ra.One* had taken the hit. This cryptic status added fuel to the *Ra.One-Bodyguard* jokes doing the rounds. Many wondered whether the comment was Alvira's brainchild or whether it was Salman who had put her up for it. Of course, those close to the Khan sister claimed it was just a joke and not meant to hurt anyone.

The several-year-long fight came to an end at Baba Siddique's iftar party, when Salman hugged Shah Rukh. It was a Ramzan party, an occasion for sharing and spreading goodness and brotherhood. So letting bygones be bygones, Salman hugged Shah Rukh and he responded with equal warmth. Both actors later said that they always considered each other family, and that their fight was blown out of proportion by the media.

'Like all boys, we have a lot of energy and intensity in our relationship. Sometimes, it is friction; sometimes, it is fun and sporty. We hug, we huddle and we fight,' shared Shah Rukh in an interview with ABP News in 2018.

In 2014, Shah Rukh dropped in at Arpita's sangeet ceremony. The picture of Arpita endearingly sandwiched between Shah Rukh and Salman made it to the headlines.

On 26 May 2015, Shah Rukh surprised millions of fans,

when he tweeted—'I believe being a brother is bigger than being a hero. "Bhaijaan" coming Eid 2015. How do u like the first look?'—promoting the much-awaited first look of Salman's upcoming *Bajrangi Bhaijaan*. He soon made a guest appearance in Salman's *Tubelight* and more than once joined Salman on the small-screen reality show *Bigg Boss*. Incidentally, this show, which is synonymous with Salman, was initially offered to Shah Rukh, but he could not work out his dates. Today, Shah Rukh confesses that the connect Salman has with the contestants and the audience is phenomenal and irreplaceable.

Much later, sometime in 2018, when Shah Rukh had finished the first schedule of *Zero* and was brainstorming with director Anand Rai, he got a call from Salman at 2:30 a.m. Salman came over to his house with two new Being Human e-cycles. One for Aryan and one for Suhana.

Salman then casually asked, '*Arrey, picture shuru kar di*? (Oh, you have started the film?).' When Shah Rukh told him that they had shot for ten days and were now thinking of doing a song, Salman immediately said, '*Mai karunga* (I will do it).' He quickly asked one of his staff, '*Kab hai tarikh*? (When are my dates free?)' Then turning to Shah Rukh, he said, '3rd, 4th, 5th are free. *Ho jayega*? (3rd, 4th, 5th are free. Can it be done?)' And the two Khans shared screen space in a full song in *Zero*.

'*Mere Karan Arjun aayenge* (My Karan Arjun will come back)' well defines the brotherhood and brawls of two of the biggest stars of B-town. Today, the two of them seem to have sealed their relationship with maturity and share a much stronger bond than they ever did.

'Karan Arjun' have finally arrived.

Rising from the Ashes

(December 2013. The rapid-fire round on a television chat show over exotic coffee.)

Host: Rate yourself as a father on 10.
Aamir: 5 on 10.
Host: Husband?
Aamir: 5 on 10.
Host: Actor?
Aamir: 5 on 10.
Host: Are you on a loop or are you okay?
Aamir: No, no. All 5 on 10. Abhi tak toh five hi chal raha hai *(It's all 5 till now).*
Host: As a director?
Aamir: 5 on 10.
Host (a little exasperated): You are a mid-level everything?
Aamir: I genuinely feel I am mid-level.
Host: In bed?
Aamir: (surprised) In bed? You are seriously asking me? God knows, yaar. That you ask her (pointing to wife, Kiran Rao) Why are you asking me?
(Kiran and Aamir laugh)
Host (to Kiran): You say.
Kiran (with a naughty smile): It's his tough question. Why should I answer?

Aamir (extremely embarrassed): Good god! 5 on 10. Bed also 5 on 10. 50/50.
Kiran (adds vehemently): Not 5 on 10. It's more.
Aamir: Chalo. Thank you (smiles and still embarrassed).

Aamir had finally found a happy place in his relationship with Kiran. But that does not take away from his agonizing story and the suffering he had had to battle through to reach this point of equilibrium.

Although Aamir rang in the millennium with celebrations of successful films such as *Lagaan* and *Dil Chahta Hai*, it was sadly a time of agony too.

Aamir's marriage, a companionship of sixteen years, with his childhood sweetheart, Reena, had ended in separation and eventually in divorce. Both maintained a dignified silence with a public statement, which was the divorce petition that stated, 'Irreconcilable differences arose between them on account of temperamental differences, making it impossible for them to live together.'[43]

Rumours that linked the actor to his *Dil Chahta Hai* co-star Preity Zinta were afloat. Some of them even reported him to be secretly married to her. With all this strife around him, the reticent Aamir went into a shell and complete isolation.

Aamir would lock himself up in a dark room and not interact with anyone. He would keep awake all night and drink an entire bottle of Bacardi to drown his sorrows. His friend

---

[43]Anand Sonndas, 'It's lagan to end an innings', *The Telegraph*, 9 December 2002, accessed 23 September 2019, https://www.telegraphindia.com/india/it-s-lagan-to-end-an-innings-aamir-khan-and-wife-reena-file-for-divorce/cid/964622

Ameen Haji (the best man in Aamir's second wedding and co-star who played the role of Bagha, the mute drummer in *Lagaan*) sat with him through many a night like this. Aamir would talk non-stop about whatever had happened in his life. On one such night, Ameen recalls drawing the example of Guru Dutt with Aamir. Aamir agreed with his friend that even Dutt in his depressive state had taken refuge in alcohol, but that had finally ended in his suicide. Ameen told him firmly, 'This is not how I see you ending up and we will not let this happen to you. I will not stand here and watch you fall.' The next morning, Aamir assured his friend that he had given it a thought and would work on it.

During this time, his one-time 4 a.m. friend, Juhi Chawla, with whom he had had a falling-out during the filming of *Ishq*, called him. She had not spoken to him for years. But now, she felt, was the time to reach out to her friend. She had seen Aamir's love for Reena blossom during the *Qayamat Se Qayamat Tak* days. She knew how important the relationship was for Aamir and tried hard to talk to him to help mend his broken heart.

But the drinking did not stop.

This was also the time Aamir bonded with his once co-star, Salman. 'He walked into my life at a juncture when I was at my lowest. I was going through a very bad phase after my separation and divorce. For about a year and a half, I was just locked up in my house and on a downslide. That's when I bumped into him again and he said he wanted to come over. He did, and we started drinking. I was drinking a lot at that time, I don't know how, but something connected there. It kind of grew, we began spending more time together', remembers Aamir. Salman's support and bonding helped him regain his spirit to a large extent.

But the one phone call that had the most impact on Aamir was an unexpected one. It was from an assistant director of his film, *Lagaan*—Kiran Rao. Aamir had met Kiran on the sets of *Lagaan*. She was one of the many assistants of Ashutosh Gowariker. They were not even friends and she was just another member of the unit. After his separation, during this most traumatic phase, she called him and the conversation they had, lasted for over half an hour. When he put the phone down, he remembers saying to himself, 'My god! I feel so happy when I talk to her!'

After that phone call, Aamir wanted to meet and interact more with Kiran. She had infused in him a new sense of cheer and purpose. Aamir and Kiran started meeting up and very soon they began dating. Their courtship took a turn towards commitment when they decided to live-in together. Aamir and Kiran stayed together for more than a year. And then three years after his separation from first wife, Reena, they were married on 28 December 2005.

After the wedding, the family headed for Panchgani, near Mumbai. It was a three-day celebration that culminated in a grand reception and was attended by several celebrities from all walks of life. Aamir, it was reported, enjoyed the occasion and was in a relaxed mood. He played cricket and tennis with his friends. This was his way of recreating the ambience of the days when he was filming *Laagan*—the film on the cricket match between the British officials and the villagers, where he had first met Kiran. This was followed by a low-profile wedding reception at the Bangalore Club hosted by Kiran's parents. Aamir, dressed in a black suit, and Kiran, dressed in a white saree with a golden border, looked the perfect match as they interacted with the guests.

Aamir confesses now, 'I can never imagine a life without Kiran as my partner. I feel very blessed and I am very grateful that she is such a wonderful person.'

In the Media Spotlight

The first half of the millennium brought in joy for Aamir but not without its fair share of gossip and controversies that screamed celebrity slander. Come September 2005, and *Stardust* magazine read: 'Exclusive from London–2 Year Old Jaan! The love child Aamir Khan abandoned!'[44] Aamir and Jaan both starred on the cover page.

According to the scoop revealed by the magazine, Aamir had met a British journalist, Jessica Hines, on the sets of *Ghulam*. Jessica had come to India to write a book on Amitabh Bachchan. The article reported that Aamir and Hines started living together. Things were going perfectly fine for them, till Hines got pregnant and everything changed overnight. It was alleged by the media that Hines had resisted pressure from Aamir to abort the child and decided to raise Jaan—born on 14 September 2003—all by herself. She was further quoted as having accused Aamir of not inquiring about the child even once. This child, with Indian features, later modelled on the cover of *Vogue* magazine. Today Hines is married to a London-based businessman, William Talbot, and says, 'Jaan is a happy kid. He has a daddy now in William, so why should he ask about anyone else?' However, Aamir always maintained that

---

[44]Bollywood Journalist, https://bollywoodjournalist.com/articles-i-like/supporting-pages/statement-of-stardust-editor-regarding-aamir-khan-and-jessica-hines-controversy/, accessed 18 September 2019

Sanjukta Nandy

he has fathered only three children, Junaid and Ira from Reena and Azad from Kiran.

Aamir is someone who likes to keep his private life away from the media spotlight. But that was not to be. Another set of controversies soon surrounded him in 2007. Aamir fought a tiresome custody battle for his brother, Faisal Khan, with his father, Tahir Hussain. It was appealed to the court that Faisal was not in sound mental health and needed supervised living. In the midst of it, Faisal reportedly accused Aamir of keeping him captive in his house, forcibly giving him medicines and pronouncing him mentally ill. The entire episode blew out of proportion and it ended up being a long drawn-out battle in court. At this time, in a public announcement, Reena's voice joined in with twenty-two members of Aamir's family to support Aamir. Reena, along with the family, condemned the comments and allegations that Tahir Hussain (who was now remarried and had a second family) and Faisal had made against Aamir. The court gave the custody of Faisal first to his father, but later it went to Aamir, as Hussain moved the court saying he was unable to take care of his younger son and that his custody should be given to his elder son, Aamir, instead. In 2008, the Bandra Metropolitan Magistrate's Court announced that Faisal need not be in anyone's custody and could live anywhere he wanted to. Since then, Faisal lives by himself in a rented apartment in the suburbs of Mumbai. In 2019, after a long sabbatical, Faisal signed a couple of Hindi films. But he mostly works in Aamir's company as a script doctor who reads and screens all new scripts offered to the company. He admits that he sits during narrations and is involved in the process of evaluation of scripts for Aamir Khan Productions.

Come June 2009 and Aamir had some more news of

unexpected turbulence coming his way. Kiran's pregnancy became public news when she was admitted to Breach Candy Hospital. Soon, Aamir wrote on his blog, 'We lost our baby.' Kiran's miscarriage led to the couple going through an emotional downhill, but they held onto each other. Aamir took a break to spend time with Kiran and helped her grow stronger, emotionally.

Separating Personal from Professional

In 2011, Kiran Rao made her directorial debut with the film *Dhobi Ghat*, which was released internationally as *Mumbai Diaries*. But she was probably the only debuting director who had outright refused to cast Aamir in her film.

When Aamir had heard her script, the superstar expressed his interest to act in her film, but Kiran said a straight 'no.' She wanted to make a low-budget film, to be shot organically, with a small crew and without attracting much attention. She was certain it could not be done that way if she was to shoot with Aamir. She presumed he would come with an entourage and the film would gather a mammoth scale in production and would gather humungous crowd and media attention. Thus, she started auditioning other actors for the role, but showed Aamir the tapes. But Aamir was not one to give up. 'Though I was rejected for the role, I put forward a proposal. I told her that she should let me do a reading so she could see the facets that this character could project. My craft was to turn into another person. I would not be Aamir, but the character,' said Aamir.

Aamir was shooting for *Ghajini* in Hyderabad and he asked Kiran to come over to Hyderabad for a screen test that he had planned for the character he wanted to play in *Dhobi Ghat*.

Once she saw the nuances and the dimensions Aamir brought to the character, she was stumped. She had looked for these elements in many actors but finally, she decided that only Aamir would play the role.

Kiran was nervous about directing Aamir in *Dhobi Ghat*, where he played the role of Arun, a reclusive artist. She knew, his would be a formidable presence on the set, and as a first-time director, it would not be easy to assert her position as the captain of the ship. Unable to cope with the pressure, she did something strange. She sought refuge in the comfort of her personal equation with him. She started to shout and snap at him. She listened to everybody's suggestions, except his. In fact, she asked him to simply shut up. Caught by surprise, Aamir was in tears on the first day of the shoot. He was so upset that he told her he could not work with her if she did not treat him the way she treated the other actors on the set. For the first few days of the shoot, they found it impossible to settle into an equation that was comfortable, yet professional. This created stress in their personal relationship as well. But gradually, Kiran realized that she did not have to be aggressive to assert her view as the director and amicably ironed out the kinks in the process.

Aamir had promised Kiran that he would not attract attention from the crowd. He worked out a strategy to keep his word. While shooting, Aamir secretly locked himself in a third-floor apartment on Mohammed Ali Road, Mumbai, where the film was being shot. The apartment had just one room and a bathroom. During the shoot, producer Vidhu Vinod Chopra and director Rajkumar Hirani visited Aamir to discuss the script of their film, *3 Idiots*. Shooting for *Dhobi Ghat* would go on in the room and these discussions would then be held in the bathroom. Vinod Chopra would sit on the commode, while Hirani and Aamir would have brainstorming sessions in the remaining space of the bathroom.

Aamir is known to cry if his film is a hit. He also cries if it fails. *Dhobi Ghat* was a labour of Kiran's and Aamir's love and the below-average box-office performance of the film gave the couple a heartache.

Agony and ecstasy followed a sinusoidal graph in Aamir's life. In 2011, a son was born to Kiran and Aamir through in vitro fertilization (IVF) surrogacy. As public figures in a country with conservative views on surrogacy, this was a bold move taken by the couple. Breaking away from common practice, they named their newborn Azad Rao Khan. Azad's name, embedded with the surnames of both his parents, was a subtle declaration of the bond of equality that the couple shared.

After Azad was born, Aamir admits that Kiran spoke to him about the fact that Aamir wasn't dedicating sufficient time to his family. One day, she sat him down and said, 'You don't really care for us. We don't exist for you. We are not even in your periphery. Even when you are with us, your mind is somewhere else. I know you love us, but yes, I am not sure if I want to change you, because then you won't be the person I fell in love with.'

Aamir understood the point she was making. From that day, whenever he was in town, he came home by 6 p.m. and spent two hours with Azad. He would give him a bath, have a family dinner, read out a story and then leave for his meetings and work.

Aamir remained close to his other children, Junaid and Ira, as well. He compliments Reena, their mother, for their upbringing, saying, 'Reena is extremely important and is very much a part of the family and she will always be. I think the bond that we share is not going to break with a piece of paper. I am lucky that I had the opportunity to be with her for sixteen years. That enriched me and we grew up together. We were very young when we got married. I give value to that and I'm glad that she does too.'

Aamir proposed a heart-warming toast on Reena's fiftieth birthday, which was attended by Kiran too. Reena and Kiran share a relationship of mutual respect and camaraderie. They are seen together on family occasions and at shoots too. The picture of Aamir's sensible modern family seemed complete.

Kiran and Aamir, on a recent chat show[45], when questioned on his multiple roles:
Aamir: Ghar pe main ghulam hoon *(I am the slave at home).*
Kiran looks amused.
Host (to Kiran): What is the one thing you would like to change about Aamir?
Kiran (with a smile): That he should bathe more frequently.
Aamir (laughs): Sher kabhi mu nahi dhota *(A tiger never washes his face).*

Both break into squeals of laughter that resonate with a promise of friendship and understanding that makes them stick together as a couple.

The duo had cracked the code of being together.

---

[45]*Point Blank* with Aamir Khan and Kiran Rao (interviewed by Sudhir Chaudhary, Live India, 31 January 2011, accessed 24 September 2019, https://www.youtube.com/watch?v=DaZAbzyhG5M

KHANtastic

18

The Baazigar 2.0

'I cried for hours,' said Shah Rukh Khan.

Ra.One, the magnum opus of 2011, an eagerly awaited Diwali release, failed to light up the charts. The film released simultaneously in Hindi, Tamil and Telugu versions in over 3,100 theatres pan India. In comparison, Salman's *Bodyguard* released a few months earlier, only in Hindi, and across 2,750 theatres. Despite a promotional onrush by Shah Rukh himself, the sci-fi opus collected ₹18.5 crore at the box office on day one, which was ₹3 crore less than collections of Salman's *Bodyguard* on day one only[46]. Media pundits immediately announced loud and clear that in the race of the Khans, who were still not on good terms then, the Bodyguard had beaten the Superhero.

As a child, Shah Rukh loved playing the man in a cape. He went on to become an actor, an entrepreneur and a gizmo aficionado. But the child in him still dreamed of being in the shoes of the superhero. That's how Ra.One was born.

[46]Nandini Raghavendra, '*Ra.One*: Shahrukh Khan's movie turns a profit in 3 days', *The Economic Times*, 29 October 2011, accessed 24 September 2019, https://economictimes.indiatimes.com/industry/media/entertainment/ra-one-shahrukh-khans-movie-turns-a-profit-in-3-days/articleshow/10528725.cms?from=mdr

A Superhero Flies the Odds

Shah Rukh's mantra had always been to gamble with high odds. The fact that he was one of the few mainstream lead actors who started off with playing negative characters was in itself a reflection of his secure and confident persona. Thus, Shah Rukh invested his hard-earned money and produced mega-budget films such as *Phir Bhi Dil Hai Hindustani* and *Aśoka*. These films did not rake in high profits, but that did not deter his aspirations to continue making the kind of films that he wanted to.

But perhaps he knew that he would first need to travel the beaten path and garner money. Hence, in 2003, Shah Rukh took over the defunct production company Dreamz Unlimited, which he had created with Juhi Chawla and director Aziz Mirza in 1999, and launched *Main Hoon Na*, the directorial debut of friend Farah Khan in 2004. The company transformed into Red Chillies Entertainment, Gauri Khan became the producer and the film went on to become hugely successful. In 2007, Farah directed *Om Shanti Om* for Red Chillies again, and this film, too, did exceptional business.

These successful commercial riders were enough for Shah Rukh to dive into yet another risky venture, *Ra.One*. Unusually named after the villain of the film, *Ra.One* was planned to be a mammoth, superhero fantasy, starring Shah Rukh himself. Designed to be India's answer to the world of G.I. Joe and superheroes, along with world-class visual effects and graphic innovation, the product was an expensive venture. Trade analysts called it a huge gamble, but Shah Rukh was sure, 'I'll convince people that a man in tights can fly in India...'

Unfortunately for Shah Rukh, the flight did not take off.

The film was a dud and according to *The Economic Times*, he went bankrupt.[47] It seemed like it was all over for Shah Rukh Khan, the producer.

But in an interview to *Filmfare*, he held his head high and said,

> I did go a little wrong with *Ra.One*. It made 172 crores at the box-office but still, people call it a wrong film. It went wrong because it was different. I was depressed for three months after the release of the film. As a matter of fact, till date I'm depressed and upset. But around fifteen days ago, I made up my mind to make a 300 crore film and silence everyone. It's not in anger or madness. It was nice to go wrong.[48]

This is probably because Shah Rukh, the producer, continues to dream on. He says he wants to give something back to the industry that has made him the star that he is. Not only the movies, but Shah Rukh also wanted to do something in the scope of his first love—sports.

Since his early days, Shah Rukh was inclined towards football. Although prone to getting hurt, it didn't stop him from playing. His coach in school, Singh saab, used to say that Shah Rukh could play even if his legs were chopped off. But Shah Rukh's dream of wanting to be a sportsman was cut

---

[47]"Stars who lost their money as fast as they earned it', *The Economic Times*, 7 August 2017, accessed 24 September 2019, https://economictimes. indiatimes.com/industry/media/entertainment/stars-who-lost-their-money-as-fast-as-they-earned-it/raj-kapoor/slideshow/59951365.cms

[48]Rahul Gangwani, 'I cried for hours – SRK', Filmfare.com, 11 December 2012, accessed 24 September 2019, https://www.filmfare.com/interviews/i-cried-for-hours-srk-1884.html

Sanjukta Nandy

short by a terrible back injury at school. However years later, it was this incomplete ambition that inspired him to buy the Kolkata Knight Riders (KKR).

Shah Rukh remembers when Lalit Modi, the first chairman and commissioner of the Indian Premier League (IPL), and members from his team had met him with their plans to start a cricket league, all he kept saying was that he wanted a football team. Modi said, 'Start with cricket and then we will make the soccer team.'

The IPL auction, to decide the owners, set a base price for the franchises at $400 million. At the end of the auction, the franchises were sold for a total of $723.59 million. After bidding for his IPL team, Shah Rukh lay awake all night, hoping that the bid would not get accepted. The stakes were high and he had no money at that time to pay for it. The bid, however, went through. KKR was bought by Shah Rukh's company Red Chillies Entertainment in partnership with actress Juhi Chawla and her husband, Jay Mehta, for a price of $75.09 million. Although Shah Rukh managed to pull off the bid, he knew the test had just started. To keep afloat financially, KKR would have to win the games. The anthem for the team became, *'Korbo, Lorbo, Jeetbo re* (We will perform, fight and win).'

Shah Rukh's team fared poorly and lost for four long years. To keep their morale high, and his own, Shah Rukh kept cheering them from the stands match after match. Soon, Shah Rukh's family told him to sell off KKR. They said it was only bringing in negativity. Fortunately, he stood by his commitment and was rewarded, when the team finally won the trophy in its fifth year, in 2012, defeating Chennai Super Kings (CSR) who were the favourites. An ecstatic Shah Rukh said, 'The world at large lynched me, year after year, for four consecutive years.

They completely destroyed me. But I'm glad I didn't sell it. I needed to win. That's why I didn't quit. And I am still waiting for the soccer team they promised me, now that my cricket team is doing well.' Shah Rukh was finally in a happy place.

But the vicious tentacles of controversy were just warming up to take over his life once again.

No More Squabbles

It was 16 May 2012. Wankhede Stadium, Mumbai. The IPL tournament was in full swing. The match was between Mumbai Indians, the local favourites, and KKR. Shah Rukh reached the stadium at around 11:45 p.m. His team was winning and all was well.

After the match, Shah Rukh, his team and family were in a celebratory mood. Shah Rukh's son, Aryan and daughter, Suhana had reached the stadium with a group of twenty-odd friends. The ecstatic kids were dancing below the dressing room. The security guard at Wankhede Stadium, Vikas Dalvi, asked the children to move away. When Shah Rukh saw this, he told the guard that they were with him. Then he told his business manager, Karuna Badwal, to take the children out of the stadium. This incident triggered a volley of arguments, which not only ruined Shah Rukh's mood of celebration but also set the premise for a fight. As the temperature of the arguments rose, fuel was added to fire when reportedly an official started abusing Shah Rukh. This irked the Khan and instigated him further. Finally, the control on his patience gave way and Shah Rukh started fighting in public. Mumbai Cricket Association (MCA) members and the chief operating officer (COO) of IPL, Sundar Raman, reached the spot, along with Mumbai Police officer, ACP Iqbal Sheikh. Sheikh asked both the parties to cool down and soon after Shah Rukh left the venue. A complaint was registered against him with the police. He was accused of being drunk and heatedly arguing on the grounds. Shah Rukh denied any allegation of being drunk. He also denied having used abusive language. In his statement to the police on 23 June 2012, he stated that all pictures and sounds of the incident uploaded on various sites over the Internet did not belong to him. Also, as the children were already in the custody of Badwal, there was no foul word uttered in front of them.

Dalvi's statement was recorded by Mumbai Police on 27 June 2012. He said that on that evening around twenty kids were walking towards the pitch when he blew the whistle and asked them to stop. He asked the children to leave the ground. At that moment, Shah Rukh and a few of his friends got angry and charged at the security guard. The guard was attacked and abused. It was only after Sheikh's intervention that Shah Rukh and his friends left the venue. Dalvi also stated that although there was no foul language used in front of the children, he could not confirm if Shah Rukh was in an inebriated condition at the time.

After the incident, Vilasrao Deshmukh, the then MCA president, banned Shah Rukh from entering the Wankhede Stadium for five years. Deshmukh was quoted to have said, 'The managing committee of the MCA at its meeting today has condemned the behaviour of Shah Rukh Khan, who without any provocation hurled abuses at MCA officials and manhandled the security guard in the presence of BCCI-IPL officials.'[49]

[49]Parabjeet Singh Sethi, '#ThrowbackThursday: When Shah Rukh Khan was

Within three years, in 2015, this five-year ban was revoked by the then MCA president, Sharad Pawar. In a statement, MCA vice-president, Ashish Shelar, had said, 'Today, in the meeting, it was decided that the ban imposed on Kolkata franchise owner Shah Rukh Khan should be lifted. With the prior approval of our president Sharad Pawar, it was proposed by me that the ban on him be lifted, and the managing committee approved it unanimously.'[50]

After extensive investigation, Mumbai Police too concluded that Shah Rukh was not drunk and did not use abusive language before minors at Wankhede Stadium on that fateful night of 2012.

After the incident, Shah Rukh's wife, Gauri, and son, Aryan, had sat him down and spoken to him. Their counsel calmed down the fuming Khan and he was remorseful of his public outburst. Shah Rukh had said, 'I am a peaceful person by nature. I never raise my voice even at home. So, my children got scared when they saw me getting angry at the stadium.' He agreed that it was 'not cool to lose his cool'. However, he justified that he had lost control on his patience this time, as the matter involved offhand ungraciousness towards children and that he was overtly sensitive in this matter. Additionally, the uncivil abuses hurled at him during the argument had hints

---

banned from the Wankhede Stadium for five years', t2online, 22 March 2018, accessed 30 September 2019, http://t2online.com/sport/throwbackthursday-when-shah-rukh-khan-was-banned-from-the-wankhede-stadium-for-five-years/cid/19081

[50]PTI, 'MCA lifts ban on Shahrukh Khan, but won't support Ankeet Chavan', *The Economic Times*, 2 August 2015, accessed 24 September 2019, https://economictimes.indiatimes.com/news/sports/mca-lifts-ban-on-shahrukh-khan-but-wont-support-ankeet-chavan/articleshow/48316942.cms?from=mdr

of communal bias, ridiculing his religious faith, and this had further aggravated his fury. After this outburst, Shah Rukh promised to himself that if he ever got as angry as this again, he would lock himself up in the bathroom and vent his anger but would never do so in a public space. No more storms, squabbles and dissensions, however challenging the situation is, promised Shah Rukh to himself and even said so in his interviews there on.

But what could Shah Rukh do when trouble once again came knocking on his door without provocation? This time he kept his cool and spent good time catching Pokemons while being detained by the United States authorities at the Los Angeles International Airport in 2016. It was not the first time, that United States immigration had detained the Khan.

In 2009, Shah Rukh was detained by United States immigration at the Newark Liberty International Airport in New Jersey for about two hours after his name came up on a terror-alert list. Ironically, he was travelling to the country to publicize his film *My Name Is Khan*, which was about the racial profiling of Muslims.

Once again, he was detained in 2012 at the Westchester County Airport near New York, while travelling in a private jet with Nita Ambani, wife of business magnate, Mukesh Ambani. At that time, the star had been invited to deliver a lecture at Yale University and consequently he reached the venue three hours late.

Shah Rukh subsequently addressed the gathering at the university with his inherent wit and confessed, 'Whenever I start feeling too arrogant about myself, I always take a trip to America. The immigration guys kick the star out of stardom.'

He also tweeted: 'I fully understand and respect security

with the way the world is. But to be detained by the United States Immigration every damn time, really, really sucks.' Strangely, it was a case of mistaken identity, as his name and date of birth happened to exactly match that of a person on America's watch list. The only consolation that Shah Rukh could perhaps derive from these incidents was that he was not alone. His friend, Aamir, too was interrogated and searched at the Chicago International Airport, way back in 2002.

Shah Rukh's jollity, a signature approach of the Khan, did create another controversy for him, this time with Aamir. Aamir wrote in his blog, 'I'm sitting under a tree, on the edge of a valley, approximately 5000 feet above sea level. Ammi, Ira and Junaid are by my side and we are in the middle of one of our favourite board games. Shah Rukh is licking my feet and I am feeding him biscuits every now and then. What more can I ask for?' Aamir signed off the blog with. 'Shah Rukh is once again begging for my attention, so let me get back to him. He is smelling too much. I think he needs a bath. Heel Boy, heel.'[51]

This information went viral. Aamir's blog dishevelled a major part of the Shah Rukh fan following and the press. The media directed the spotlight on the Khans' animosity. Aamir stated that he had been working in the industry for over twenty years and had never commented on anyone, but lately, he had noticed that Shah Rukh had been regularly commenting on him. Aamir said that he is never the first to comment, but he does respond once in a while. He then went on to clarify that he was referring to his pet dog Shah Rukh, who stayed

---

[51]Aamirkhan.com, accessed 24 September 2019, http://www.aamirkhan.com/blog/login.php?topicid=402&show=1&page=30

in his Panchgani holiday home, and not Shah Rukh Khan. Aamir added that when he had bought the house, the dog was already staying in it. Apparently, Shah Rukh was shooting a commercial in the same Panchgani house a few years ago, and the caretakers of the house had bought this pup and hence named him after the then rising star.

Once matters turned ugly, Aamir came over to Shah Rukh's house to clear the air. Aamir spoke to Shah Rukh and his children and explained that it was just a blog written in light humour that had escalated to an immense proportion. He had no intention to hurt their feelings and regretted if he had done so. Shah Rukh went on to say, 'I have never bothered about it because I also say a lot of things in fun and I think I may be stressing somebody else out. I don't get stressed when friends pass comments like this. Actually, I enjoy it.' All was resolved. When asked to comment on this episode later, Shah Rukh, swift with his wit, was quick to add with a naughty twinkle in his eyes, 'I do not eat biscuits anymore.'

Pati Patni aur Woh?

Misunderstood quotes and bizarre events snowballing overnight have all been synonymous with Shah Rukh. But his family life with Gauri and the children stood rock solid through the tempest. Until one day, when his name was linked with a young, dusky, Miss India World winner. Ironically, when she was being crowned, years ago, Shah Rukh was part of the jury and he had asked her about her choice of husband in the question-answer (Q&A) round. Her name was Priyanka Chopra.

Years later, Shah Rukh and Priyanka starred in *Don* and *Don 2* together and went on record to admit that they

185

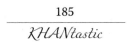

shared a 'unique friendship', which was beyond anybody's comprehension. 'Personally, I am quite uncomfortable around actors. I get very conscious. But Priyanka makes me feel comfortable. She'll fix my hair if it's out of place. It's nice working with a friend like that. Also, she has realised that I am as insecure as anyone else.'

Shah Rukh and Priyanka often went on tours to host shows together and travelled to film festivals. All this panned out as regular work demands. Rumours started brewing when the film fraternity had to invite Priyanka to their parties just on Shah Rukh's request. Sounds of disgruntlement began building up within Shah Rukh's inner circle too. Instances such as Shah Rukh's special treatment towards Priyanka, wherein he recommended her to producers or her frequent visits to Mannat, were pointed out to allege an affair.

After *Don 2*, rumours about Shah Rukh and Priyanka gained momentum and Gauri was reportedly not happy about it. Their alleged relationship was much deliberated especially when Priyanka was spotted coming out of Shah Rukh's office at 3 a.m. once. Both maintained that they were rehearsing for the Zee Cine Awards. But speculation about their relationship reached its peak.

So intense were the waves of these rumours, that it was said that Gauri was taken aback by the situation. In a bid to protect their hard-earned reputation and public love, Shah Rukh had to say goodbye to Priyanka, who had by now become an irreplaceable part of their closest friend circle. Shah Rukh had said in a TV interview,

> To me, what is most disturbing is the fact that a lady who has worked with me has been questioned, and somewhere

down the line, not been shown the kind of respect I show her, and all other women. I think it's a little disrespectful. I am extremely sorry about that. Sorry not because of anything I have done, but the fact that she is my friend. She is one of the closest friends I have and very close to my heart and always will be. I just feel that sometimes when things are said, I need to step back from it because I find it very small and menial and it just tends to spoil the relationship that people share while working together. We have shared some of the nicest moments on-screen, off it as friends and it's unfortunate. It's sad for me to think that a friendship gets a little soiled.

Stories and speculations about this relationship again went viral when Priyanka appeared in an international chat show called *Dirty Laundry with Laura Brown*. Priyanka candidly spoke about her past relationships and flaunted a Dolce & Gabbana leather airport jacket stating that it belonged to an ex-boyfriend and had stayed with her. She mentioned that it was her favourite jacket and that she literally lived in it while travelling. Ironically, images of Shah Rukh wearing a similar jacket in the past popped up in social media, with the Twitteratti speculating about the alleged relationship once again.

In 2013, AbRam was born to Shah Rukh and Gauri through surrogacy, bringing in a bounty of sunshine into their family. Priyanka steered westward to Hollywood and later married singing star Nick Jonas in 2018.

Shah Rukh faced an avalanche of trials and tribulations on professional and personal front. But he was not the kind of person who quits midway. His philosophy was: 'Throw me to a pack of wolves and I will return leading the pack.'

19

Return of the Khans

*N*ew York hardly ever has a power cut. But it happened once in 2004.

The atmosphere was taut as Paul Aponte, personal security of an actor, was moving ahead with a cell phone torch through a hotel hallway. It was dark and the hallway had an eerie tunnel-like feel. As Paul measured forth his footsteps carefully, out came a hand from the dark and grabbed him. A man in a towel was frantically asking for help as he felt he was about to have a heart attack. Paul helped the man and gave him first aid. But he still held on to his chest complaining of severe discomfort. At that moment of emergency, they heard footsteps in the corridor. A young movie star was walking past them.

The man forgot his discomfort, stood up in his towel and started screaming in excitement, 'Shah Rukh! Shah Rukh!' Paul was scared that the man might now truly have a heart attack. Later he remarked that he had been in the security service for long and had seen numerous fan reactions, even around a star as big as Brad Pitt, but never before had he seen such hysteria it surrounded this Khan.

If Shah Rukh could resurrect an almost dead man to life, he could do it to his failing career too.

After the debacle of *Ra.One*, Yash Chopra came to him with yet another love story. Chopra was collaborating with his favourite actor after eight long years and this one was touted to be his magnum opus, *Jab Tak Hai Jaan*, wherein Shah Rukh was to play a bomb-disposal specialist. The director-actor duo decided to pull out all stops for this one.

Shah Rukh had an unsaid rule. He never kissed his leading ladies on screen. But *Jab Tak Hai Jaan* had a kiss between Katrina Kaif and him. Chopra explained to him why it was necessary for the film, and Shah Rukh could not give this a miss. Shah Rukh and Chopra put in their best efforts for *Jab Tak Hai Jaan* to rule the box office. The release was made to coincide with Chopra's golden jubilee year in Bollywood. It was his twenty-second and final film as a director before he passed away on 21 October 2012, a month before the film released. Shah Rukh lost a father figure. But Chopra had given Shah Rukh his biggest gift before departing. Come Diwali, 2012, and *Jab Tak Hai Jaan* had a cracker run.

In 2013, came a *Dilwale Dulhania Le Jayenge*-inspired comical drama from the *Golmaal* series director, Rohit Shetty. And who else other than Shah Rukh to play Rahul, the lead for Rohit Shetty's, *Ready Steady Po*? To highlight the train sequence, when Shah Rukh meets the leading lady for the first time, and to retain the South Indian flavour of the film, it was eventually renamed *Chennai Express*. Kareena Kapoor was the first choice for the role, but she was busy shooting *Talaash* with yet another Khan. So in stepped Deepika Padukone, who had already had a successful stint with Shah Rukh in *Om Shanti Om*. It released on International Women's Day and on Shah Rukh's insistence, Deepika was credited ahead of the actor in the titles of the film. Shah Rukh further declared that henceforth, in his films, the leading lady's name will always precede his.

Chennai Express surprised everyone with its overwhelming response. The film superseded the collections of Aamir's *3 Idiots*, making a gross collection of ₹395 crore worldwide.[52] Shah Rukh Khan was back. He was bigger and better.

Those who grew up in the 1990s witnessed the meteoric rise of Shah Rukh. He was one from the crowd, a commoner who worshipped stars, but in a matter of a few years, became one. Perhaps there never will be another success story like his.

Does Shah Rukh ever fear losing his stardom?

Years ago, when Shah Rukh was shooting for *Rab Ne Bana Di Jodi* (in 2008) and he had changed his look to that of a mild-mannered office worker with well-oiled hair, spectacles and a moustache, he realized that people on the sets passed by him with no sense of recognition. 'I have got a taste of things to come thirty years later, when I am no longer a star. But I hope it never happens to me, ever.'

Salmania is Born

Kyon Ki...—Flop
Shaadi Karke Phas Gaya Yaar—Flop
Jaan-E-Mann—Flop
Baabul—Flop
Salaam-e-Ishq—Flop
Partner—Hit

[52]Accessed 24 September 2019, https://www.bollymoviereviewz.com/2013/08/chennai-express-box-office-collection.html

Marigold—Flop
God Tussi Great Ho—Flop
Hello—Flop
Yuvraj—Flop

This is what Salman's filmography read from end of 2005 to mid-2009. The writing was on the wall. The Salman magic seemed to be over.

Salman realized that the need of the hour was to redefine himself. The romantic hero needed to step back and create an appeal that was macho and universal.

Producer Boney Kapoor remembers the day when the idea was put into action. Salman and he had sat together and watched the Telegu hit, *Pokiri*. Salman agreed to do the Hindi remake of the film, titled *Wanted*. But the next morning, a tentative Salman met Kapoor and asked him, 'Are you going to make me do the stunts myself?' Kapoor nodded a solemn yes. Salman smiled and went on to keep his commitment. After all, he believed, '*Ek bar joh maine commitment kar di... uske baad toh main khud ki bhi nahi sunta* (Once I make a commitment, I don't listen even to myself).'

This same dialogue that featured in *Wanted* brought the house down and 'houseful' boards hung outside theatres for weeks in September 2009. Prem, the romantic poster boy of *Maine Pyar Kiya*, transformed into Radhe, a gangster with a mysterious past. Salman became an action star and the chaotic fan craze, which the media termed 'Salmania', was born. *Wanted* was Salman's Eid release, and ever since, every Eid has seen a Salman film at the ticket counter.

The Eid of 2010 launched the humorous police inspector, Chulbul Pandey into the hearts of the audience with *Dabangg*, where the Khan continued to reinvent himself. He sported a thin moustache for the first time on screen.

Salman had once gone to a wedding and was dancing with his relatives when in came his happy spirited Bharat mama and started dancing, moving his belt up and down. Salman followed his steps and then hugged his uncle, saying, '*Mama, tumhara yeh step to gaya* (Uncle, I am taking this step from you).' And thus was born the iconic belt dance step of *Dabangg*.

Affectionately called 'Bhai' (or brother) or 'Bhaijaan' by his fans, Salman's well-sculpted muscles, unbuttoned shirts and hairstyles had been a style statement for generations of young male fans thronging gyms across the country. But now it was *Dabangg*'s Chulbul Pandey who was here to stay. With sunglasses perched on his back collar, Pandeyji, pushed the sale of aviators overnight.

So immense was Salman's charisma and so fanatic were his admirers by now, that all Salman needed to do was stand up and put his hands in his pockets and dance. He transformed himself to become the people's hero, a metaphor of today's Robinhood. The stardom of 'Dabangg' Khan became a heavily guarded fort held together by a cult of fans with overbrimming emotions and glorification for brand Salman.

Even Lady Luck had fallen in love with Salman. Shah Rukh, who could have been Kabir Khan's *Ek Tha Tiger*, turned it down, citing date issues. He was working on Chopra's *Jab Tak Hai Jaan* at that time and couldn't accommodate another film, even though it was produced by the same production house. Salman signed on the dotted line and roared as Tiger. This was Salman's first collaboration with Yash Raj Films, despite being in the industry for twenty-four years. The film went on to break the record for the highest first-day box-office collections ever.

Ek Tha Tiger, released in 2012, managed to enter the 100-crore club in just five days,[53] which broke the record set by Salman's own blockbusters *Bodyguard* and *Ready*, just a year earlier. The film turned out to be such an enormous hit that it went on to become a franchise. Come 2017, Salman roared louder with the collections of *Tiger Zinda Hai.*

Salman's most acclaimed Eid release of 2015 was the entertaining, yet emotionally moving *Bajrangi Bhaijaan.* It became the third-highest opening weekend for an Indian film, went on to win the National Award for Best Popular Film Providing Wholesome Entertainment and won several Indian and international awards too. Salman, who was never the critics' blue-eyed boy, finally seemed to have won them over as well.

Blockbuster after blockbuster, Salman marched on with *Sultan,* in which he played the middle-aged wrestler, who gives up the sport after his son's death only to set out once again to revive his career for the prize money and respect. Wearing the langot (or loin cloth) and wrestling in *Sultan* were the most difficult tasks Salman had to do for any role. He had requested the director if he could wear shorts instead. It was a firm 'no', as the director was certain it would take away the authenticity from the character and the film. Salman remembers,

> The walk to the shoot from my make-up-van was very embarrassing. The crowd was huge and people were calling out to me. I am not usually a shy person when it comes to taking off my shirt but this was not easy.

[53]The Telegraph online, 'Bo biggies 100 crore club', 26 June 2013, accessed 24 September 2019, https://www.telegraphindia.com/entertainment/bo-biggies-100-crore-club/cid/287634

KHANtastic

Before I had to take off my 'lungi' and be in the 'langot' for the shoot, I warned onlookers that there would be no cat calls. As soon I took off my 'lungi', there would be cheering and whistling. It was one of those moments I felt really embarrassed. Some cat calls were there behind the '*ghunghats*' (women with heads covered) and I knew they were familiar junior artists. This made it even more difficult. But it was the need of the character, so I just went with it.

The toil paid off and *Sultan* turned out to be another one of his impressive successes.

Meanwhile, even television channels wanted a pie of Salman's stardom. The star entered into Indian living rooms with the reality shows *10 Ka Dum* and *Bigg Boss*. He proved to be a host par excellence, enthralled the audience with his crackling sense of humour and the shows garnered phenomenal TRPs. With the super success of *10 Ka Dum*, Sony TV regained its third position in Indian Television ratings. Salman Khan won the Best Anchor Award at the Indian Telly Awards in 2008 and 2009.

Salman started as the main host of the reality television show of *Bigg Boss* in 2010, taking over from the fourth season of the show. His connect with the audience with his carefree magnetism and devil-may-care swag was immediate. Salman Khan and *Bigg Boss* became synonymous to each other. From 2010 to 2019, Salman ruled and continues to rule the TRP of Indian television with the show.

Salman fans were further fascinated by his relentless contribution to his non-governmental organization (NGO), Being Human. Salman formed this NGO in 2007 to provide education and healthcare services for the underprivileged in India. Being Human started off being primarily funded by the sales of their branded merchandise. With the advent of the NGO, Salman was seen at almost every private or public event dressed in his Being Human clothing, subtly promoting the growth of this institution. Salman's fans and common people now had a humanitarian reason to root for him. They also gave their hero a demigod status.

Most ₹100-crore films. Highest first-week collections. Most ₹200–300-crore grossers. Salman had it all now. But according to the Khan, himself, this had very little to do with his acting. He had once said, 'I am surviving on mediocre talent. *Bas, fan following bahut tagdi hai* (My fans are my strength).'

Aamir: The Perfectionist

In the late 1990s, Shah Rukh took up a role that Aamir had declined. Rahul Mehra of *Darr* flagged off Shah Rukh's iconic start to meteoric stardom.

It was the beginning of the millennium when Shah Rukh declined a role and Aamir gave it his nod. This lay the foundation of a milestone in Hindi films.

Bhuvan of *Lagaan*, was born.

Initially, an excited Ashutosh Gowariker, the director of *Lagaan*, had narrated the story of the film to Aamir. Aamir had come home tired after a shoot but was always willing to listen to the stories his partner in tennis, Ashu (Gowariker), came up with.

But after hearing it, the actor did not know what to make of this story about the British Raj and some villagers playing cricket. He requested Gowariker to scrap this idea. But Gowariker returned, months later, with a complete script, finalized with dialogues. Aamir could not stop reading it.

Aamir not only agreed to act in it but even decided to produce it. A gutsy financier, Jhamu Sughand, backed the project and a mammoth team was set up. With Aamir turning producer, he had a new set of responsibilities towards the project apart from being the lead actor. His wife, Reena, who had stayed miles away from the shadow of the film industry, stepped in as the producer to share his duties. New risks were taken in both the technical and the casting department. Aamir opted for sync sound[54], a relatively new sound technology then, and a cast where the only saleable star was Aamir. It was a magnum opus. The team was huge, demands were many, risks were high and more time was being taken to film the project than estimated. Reena as a producer with a limited budget was tightening the noose, while the director wanted more freedom of time and budget. Aamir remained grounded, 'If we fail, we should fail after having made an honest effort and on our own terms. Only then can we learn and go ahead.'

Fail he did not. The first public screening of *Lagaan* took place in Bhuj in June 2001. Over 800 villagers set aside the tragedy of being struck by a massive earthquake just six months earlier on 26 January 2001 and came to watch the film. They were left overwhelmed. They realized that their participation as

---

[54]The synchronized sound recording refers to sound recorded at the time of the filming of movies, thus reducing the need to dub much during post production. It helps retain the original flavour of the performance.

background artistes, standing for hours under the sun, cheering the cricket match, had a purpose that had been seamlessly woven into a magnificent story.

The worldwide premiere of *Lagaan*, with the main cast and heads of the filmmaking departments, took place in Sun City, South Africa. It was well-received there, but all were keen to know how it would fare in India. As the film neared the end of its first show in Mumbai, Gowariker's phone rang, 'Ashu, you guys don't know what you are missing,' screamed his overwhelmed sister at the other end. She turned her phone to the Indian audience in the theatre who were screaming, 'Bhuvan! Bhuvan!'

Lagaan had scored the winning run.

All over India, hundreds of newborns were named Bhuvan. In Mumbai, tickets were not available for the first ten weeks. Even Aamir was unable to buy tickets for his friends. *Lagaan* swept a basket of trophies at all Indian film awards. It became a case study in team building at the Indian Institute of Management (IIM), Indore.[55] It received thunderous applause at the Locarno International Film Festival in Switzerland. A leading European newspaper proclaimed it to be 'Miracle at the Piazza' and creative giants such as Hollywood director Roland Joffé and musician Sir Andrew Lloyd Webber heaped praises. *Lagaan* was selected as India's official entry for the Academy Awards in the category of Best Foreign Language Film. It made it to the list of the prestigious final five nominations too, but lost the trophy to the foreign film *No Man's Land*.

Three months later, come August 2001, Javed Akhtar's son,

---

[55] *The Telegraph*, Online edition, 'Bollywood goes to B-school', 23 September 2007, accessed 24 September 2019, https://www.telegraphindia.com/7-days/bollywood-goes-to-b-school/cid/1535589

Farhan Akhtar, made his directorial debut with *Dil Chahta Hai*. Farhan had wanted to cast Aamir in the lead role and had pursued the actor for a while. When he had met Aamir for a narration, Aamir had said 'yes' immediately. But as it was Farhan's debut, he wanted to figure out if the director was equipped to captain the project.

Aamir has a photographic memory. Once the actor hears a script and likes it, he remembers every bit of it. Even during the shoot, if there is any change in the script, Aamir can identify it.

During the time that *Lagaan* was being wrapped up, Aamir called Farhan. Farhan had narrated a story to him months back and Aamir requested for another narration before giving the final nod. When he heard the script again, Aamir asked Farhan if he had changed it. Farhan answered in the negative, citing that he had only done minor changes and the story remained the same. Aamir insisted that his minor changes had mounted to the script changing as a whole. Aamir reminded Farhan that when he had come to narrate for the first time, he had come with a green file. Aamir wanted Farhan to get that file for the narration. Farhan remembered that the file was at home. On Aamir's request, he got it over immediately. As Farhan and Aamir re-read the old script from the green file, Farhan realized how much the story had changed from the first read he had done with Aamir. The meticulous actor had remembered it all. Finally, the green file translated into *Dil Chahta Hai*, a successful venture on celluloid, remembered for its freshness, crisp performances and tight script.

Two very different characters—an illiterate villager and a city-bred college-going boy—were the beginning of Brand Aamir Khan, the emergence of the experimenter and the shape-shifter who could slither into any character.

Six years after Shah Rukh handed *Lagaan* on a platter to Aamir, he refused another film. Aamir again signed up for a film that was inspired by the struggle for India's independence. The film, Rakeysh Omprakash Mehra's *Rang De Basanti*—based on a story of five boys who are inspired by Indian freedom fighters and go on to fight corruption in independent India—once again met the same fate. Hugely successful at the box office, *Rang De Basanti* was nominated for Best Foreign Language Film at the 2006 British Academy of Film and Television Arts (BAFTA) Awards, besides winning four National awards and six Filmfare awards at the 52nd Filmfare Awards in 2007, where Aamir Khan won Best Actor (Critics).

From 2006 to 2017, Aamir had a steady run of successful films and he played a new character every time. Whether it was a young college student in his early twenties from *3 Idiots* or the chiselled-bodied, violent protagonist of *Ghajini* or the athletic gymnast of *Dhoom 3*, Aamir worked hard to fit into the look of every character. For *Dhoom 3*, Aamir targeted at reducing his body fat percentage and used to hit the gym at 3 a.m., so that he could report for the shoot three hours later. After years of hard work, the actor had the same discipline that he had had in his initial days.

Aamir's dedication was noticed years ago, when he had agreed to wax his entire body to dress up as a woman for his film *Baazi*. The make-up artist, Mickey Contractor, had warned Aamir that this would hurt immensely. Contractor took it upon himself to do the job. For a minute, Aamir was numb but when the pain of waxing his chest hair engulfed him, he went blank. What followed was incessant screaming throughout the process, but never once did the dedicated Khan ask him to stop.

Aamir made his directorial debut with the sensitive film, *Taare Zameen Par*. In this film, Aamir plays the role of an unconventional Art teacher who helps a dyslexic child unravel his true hidden potential. The film was critically acclaimed and was a box-office hit.

Aamir even spent time thinking of how to create new avatars for his endorsements for Coca-Cola, Godrej, Titan, PhonePe and a host of other brands. In 2012, he hosted a television show, *Satyamev Jayate* that sought to address several social concerns. The show faced trouble, opposition and legal battles but still, it was Aamir's choice to walk the difficult path that shows his gusto.

For his 2016 film *Dangal*, he spent five months perfecting the Haryanvi dialect. The shooting schedule of the film was months away but that hadn't stopped Mr Perfectionist from piling on pounds and learning the nitty-gritties of the rustic North Indian language. He breathed life into the character of Mahavir Singh Phogat on screen and the film went on to become the biggest grosser of Hindi cinema ever.[56]

Finally, there was nothing that Aamir could not do. Come 2018, even though his magnum opus *Thugs of Hindostan*, in collaboration with Yash Raj Films, was not well-received, he remained unfazed and moved on to his next project, *Lal Singh Chaddha*. Inspired from *Lagaan*, his anthem for life is '*Chale chalo* (Keep going ahead).'

Once, when asked about the secret of his success, Aamir had said, 'What I am today is not just a result of my successes

---

[56]Web Report, City Times, 8 January 2017, accessed 24 September 2019, https://www.khaleejtimes.com/The-wrestling-film-breaks-records-set-by-three-Salman-Khan-films

Sanjukta Nandy

but also because of my failures. They taught me the most. That's why I have been able to build my career the way I have.'

On one of Shah Rukh's birthdays, a fan camouflaged as a journalist, bypassed security and sneaked into Mannat. The fan quietly made it to the private swimming pool inside the house and plunged in. After the swim, as he was wearing his clothes, the security identified the intruder and caught him. The fan remained unflustered. He said he had come to fulfil one wish. He wanted to swim in the same pool that Shah Rukh swam in. When the horrified security called the star, he asked them to bring him in. But the fan refused to meet Shah Rukh. He said his aim was only to swim in Shah Rukh's pool and his mission was accomplished. Shah Rukh asked his security to back off and the gentleman left happily. Instances of Shah Rukh's fans crossing the Sino-India border to just meet him are part of folklore.

Often, girls have barged into Salman's house, claiming to be his wife.

A fan came cycling all the way from Ranchi to Mumbai to meet his favourite star, Aamir.

Content of the film overtaking charisma of stars is the success trend for upcoming films at ticket counters today. But the footprints of the three Khans go far beyond content. The star-struck Khan fans go to the theatre to see their favourite superstar first and then perhaps search for a story. Sometimes they find it and sometimes, they are happy to just soak in the charisma of their matinee idol.

The three Khans are a reboot of the stardom commanded

by the superstars of the 1950s and '60s—the triumvirate of Raj Kapoor, Dilip Kumar and Dev Anand. They have the ability to amass the craze Rajesh Khanna had woven in the 1970s and simultaneously garner the frenzy of the Bachchan era in the 1970s and '80s. They are the 'phenomena' that picked up the relay baton of superstardom from these icons and have together ruled the hearts of millions over three decades and will probably be the last of the superstar trio on Bollywood celluloid.

Sanjukta Nandy

The Bandra Triangle

*T*he Khans of Bandra have made it to the club of landmark chapters in Bollywood history. And when the Delhi boy bought the coveted heritage property on Bandstand and named it Mannat, he completed the 'Bandra Triangle' of the Khan residences.

In August 2019, Shah Rukh was invited to launch the heritage postal stamp of Bandra Station on the completion of 130 years of the railway station. He addressed the large number of railway staffers and said he was happy to be finally on the Bandraite roster. He had become a Bandra Boy.

Salman, one of the original Bandra Boys, had once said, 'If I had done *Baazigar,* then there would be no Mannat (Shah Rukh's house) standing on Bandstand today.'

It has been debated time and again that it was Aamir's choosy nature and Salman's rejects that let Shah Rukh cement a place in the Hindi film industry. But Aamir himself says that Shah Rukh is who he is because of his genuine warmth and charisma that reaches out to people, whether it is in a room of twenty or an auditorium of 2,000 or even a stadium of 10,000 people. 'Shah Rukh Khan,' he says, 'has got that energy that you just look at him and you fall in love with him.'

It seems that all is well between the three Khans and they underscore the fact that today they have their own spaces, own lives and own films. But whenever there is a film release of any of them, the media and the trade immediately start a comparison drive, digging for new stories of competition and angst amongst them. In response, Shah Rukh retorts that the Khans don't endorse this race. When they meet up, the conversation is never about who the number one Khan is. For him, Salman is that buddy whose house he can drop in for a heart to heart, even in the middle of the night, while Aamir would be that friend he would turn to play chess with.

This warm charm was evident at a party hosted by Shah Rukh to welcome Apple CEO, Tim Cook. Aamir was invited but the perfectionist actor was on a strict diet to lose weight for his film *Dangal*. When Gauri told Aamir to not leave without having dinner, he assured her he would comply. When dinner was served, he opened his tiffin and started to eat from it. Shah Rukh and his family were shocked and they said, 'Yaar, you've come to our home and brought your own food?' Aamir explained to them that it was not a formality and he was just following his diet. The hosts easily understood.

Aamir also shares a special camaraderie with Salman, who stood by him through the darkest period of his life. Aamir was not only one of the prominent members present at Salman's sister Arpita's wedding, but he also overcame his natural shyness to dance and participate in all the wedding festivities. The Bandra Boys shared a neighbourhood in their young days but connected much later in life, only after they joined the industry. Although Aamir and Salman studied in the same class at St Anne's in Bandra for a year, they did not know each other then. Years later, when Aamir was discussing his first acting project with friend and director, Aditya Bhattacharya, at Aditya's house in Bandra, they were standing in the balcony. Salman, who also knew Bhattacharya and was cycling down

Carter Road at that time, saw them and stopped by for a chat. He told Aamir that he too was planning to become an actor. Little did they know then that they would form a constitutive part of a famous triad of actors.

Over the years, they bonded. Salman, who loves to paint, once made a painting for his friend. Aamir was deeply touched by this gesture. Aamir does quietly admit that he likes dancing to Salman's 'Dhinka chika, Dhinka chika' once in a while.

Salman once shared that Aamir and he used to go on autorickshaw rides together. Aamir never carried money and hence, Salman ended up paying every time. Aamir specially remembers one such ride when they were drunk and as usual Salman paid for the ride.

Aamir's early memory of Shah Rukh was when he was shooting on the streets of Bandra for *Raju Ban Gaya Gentleman* with Juhi Chawla. *Deewana* hadn't yet released then. Shah Rukh was amicable and well mannered. Aamir remembers the meeting fondly, not knowing at the time that the actor from Delhi would go on to become one of the superstars of the Khan trio along with Salman and him.

In 1996, Aamir and Shah Rukh had bonded when they had travelled for international shows. Shah Rukh in those days too was technologically savvy and Aamir remained slightly ignorant about gadgets. A new Toshiba computer had just emerged in the market and Shah Rukh was excited about buying it. Aamir had never used a computer in his life and asked Shah Rukh, '*Mujhe kya zaroorat hai computer ki*? (Why do I need a computer?)' Shah Rukh tried to explain to Aamir, '*Nahi, tu samajh nahi raha hai, ismein tu office daal, yeh daal woh daal...* (Please understand, you can install Microsoft Office and it will be of help).' Finally Aamir gave in. He told

Shah Rukh to go ahead and buy for him whatever he was buying for himself and hence, two identical computers were bought. Five years later when Aamir employed a new manager, the employee asked Aamir if he could use the machine, as it was just lying idle next to his desk. When the manager started the laptop, he was surprised to find that it was brand new. Aamir had never switched on the machine but didn't have the heart to stop an enthusiastic Shah Rukh from buying it.

Salman had the goodwill of always being the friend in need. In 2014, when Aamir released his film *PK* and it was surrounded by controversies, Salman chose to support him and tweeted. 'Is *PK* not an amazzziiiiing film?' Aamir too promoted Salman's *Jai Ho* on social media, posting a picture of the two urinating together and captioned it as, '*Do dost ek jhaad pe susu kartein hain toh dosti badti hai* (When two friends urinate together, they bond better), 1 day to go... Jai Ho!!!'

Aamir when asked to choose between Shah Rukh or Salman refuses to take sides. He says that they are like chalk and cheese. He defines this friendship with the example of the two borrowing cigarettes from him. Shah Rukh, he knows, would gently ask him for it, while Salman would just come, take the cigarettes and leave.

However, when Shah Rukh was told to choose between Aamir or Salman, he had a direct answer. Salman was dearer to him, without a doubt.

Salman has a humorous take on his understanding of the other two Khans. When quizzed about which actor should read a book with the title *How to Keep Your Mouth Shut*, his spontaneous reply was, 'Aamir Khan.' *How to Make Friends,* his poker-faced reply was, 'Shah Rukh Khan.' As for himself,

Sanjukta Nandy

he says he should be reading a book titled *How to Stay in a Relationship*.

Salman, Shah Rukh and Aamir are like the three vertices of a triangle. They are independent and yet just like the vertices of an equilateral triangle that connect to form one of the strongest shapes in geometry, the Khans together pack the most powerful punch in the heart of Bollywood history. The graph of their zooming successes and plunging falls have been as spiky as the stunts of a trapeze artist. Ordinary men they may be but they possess extraordinary talent to teleport the common man into a world of fantastic illusions.

KHANtastic

Epilogue

2014, Delhi.

It was the twenty-first anniversary celebration of the television show Aap ki Adalat. *The event was being attended by celebrities, movie stars, sportsmen, politicians, Prime Minister Narendra Modi and President Pranab Mukherjee. Part of the show was hosted by none other than Salman and Shah Rukh. They started with sharing witty jokes with the host, calling it* Khan ki Adalat. *The show was going well when suddenly Salman looked at his friend sitting in the audience and emotionally said into the mike,* 'Aa ja, Upar aa na, aa na *(Please come, come up on the stage, come up).' Up came Aamir on the stage. For the first time, the three Khans were on stage together. The audience broke into a thunderous applause as the three men hugged each other. History had recorded a forever moment.*

In an era when the Khans will not be there, the footprints of their journey will live on in the pixels of celluloid and their stories in the hearts of men and women.

A KHANtastic stardom that would last well past eternity.

Acknowledgements

The cover of this book bears my name, as the author, giving me credit for this entire work. But the truth is that it would not have championed into a successful manuscript without the collective assistance and dedication of an entire support system.

My husband, Kushan—my severest critic and the reader of my manuscript's first draft—I could not have done this without you. Thank you for being patient and sorry for the fights. I know there are downers when you have a headstrong writer at home who fights over every written word. I promise to be good in the time between this book and the next, but I cannot promise not to fight again during the reading of the next.

My friend and film producer, Kiran Shyam Shroff—thank you for helping me with all the aid I needed at any time of the day. Your feedback has been irreplaceable and the early morning videos of the antics of your canines were the biggest source of entertainment and respite for me during the whole time I was engrossed in the manuscript. Request you to keep them going.

Anupriya Verma, my head researcher, who worked with me for months, without a flinch or a tired grunt, going through heaps of information and tracks of audio interviews. I am quite sure she needs a much-deserved holiday for all the hard work.

All my journalist friends, especially Rekha Khan, features and entertainment editor at *Navbharat Times*, who generously gave me access to her archive of information and shared it with me. I found jewels there.

Also a big shout-out to all the journalists, experts, writers and researchers who have minutely mapped the lives of Bollywood's Khans.

My very young friend and illustrator, Rishikesh Sonawane— writing the book would not have been so much fun without you humouring me with your doodles to complement my chapter concepts. Unfortunately, the illustrations did not make it to the print due to technical reasons.

My family and friends, who understood my frenzy to work and let me disappear into the realm of words and wonder. They were always a phone call away to pep up my spirit. They were kind enough to take me back into the fold after I completed the manuscript, knowing fully well that I might disappear soon again. Thank you, my friends, for your patience, for I am one who is stubbornly not so social most of the time.

Thank you, Rupali Sebastian and Team Spojiti, for holding the fort while I was away writing my book and paid minimum attention to our assignments. Neelam Gupta, for all your help with the translations and Rupali Sonawane, for all the yummies from your restaurant that added to my prosperous adipose while I sat typing away.

My mother, for anchoring me with her calm to balance my caffeine-triggered mood swings and my mother-in-law, for monitoring the warm refills in my thermos, on my desk, even in the wee hours of the morning. My house helps for pampering me and taking care of every miniscule detail of running my home.

This book turned out the way it did because of the unconditional support of my publishing team and the editors at Rupa, who were just a phone call away at all times.

I could never end the Acknowledgements without thanking the book itself. I was so immersed in working on it that it gave me no time to grieve over my severest loss. After I finished writing the book, I realized a whole chunk of time had flown by. A book, whether you write it or read it, indeed is the best refuge.

It would not be fair to sign off without mentioning the one reading this text. Thank you for picking up the book and reading it.